Goodnight's Guide to
Great Trail Riding

*A How-to for You
and Your Horse*

By Julie Goodnight

with Heidi Nyland Melocco

Active Interest Media
d.b.a Equine Network
2520 55th Street, Suite 210
Boulder, Colo. 80301
303-625-1600
www.equisearch.com

VP, Group Publishing Director: Tom Winsor
Editorial Director: Cathy Laws
Editor: Amy Herdy

Book Design: Lauryl Eddlemon and Lara Pinson
Editor: Rene E. Riley, *The Trail Rider*
Photographs: Heidi Nyland Melocco

www.trailridermag.com

© 2011 Cruz Bay Publishing
Video © 2011 Goodnight Training Stables, Inc./Julie Goodnight

Order by calling 800-952-5813 or online at www.HorseBooksEtc.com

Library of Congress Control Number: 2011942297

Library of Congress Cataloging-in-Publication Data
Goodnight, Julie; Melocco, Heidi Nyland
Goodnight's Guide to Great Trail Riding: A How-to for You and Your Horse / by Julie Goodnight and Heidi Nyland Melocco; [photographs, Heidi Nyland Melocco].
ISBN 978-1-929164-56-1

Printed in USA

About the Authors

Julie Goodnight is an internationally known trainer, clinician, author and TV personality specializing in clear communications and effective training techniques for both horse and rider. Goodnight's diverse background and effective teaching techniques have led to her success across all disciplines of riding.

Heidi Nyland Melocco loves helping people with their horses—whether by sharing information in printed articles and photographs, producing Julie Goodnight's "Horse Master" TV show, or teaching in person (as a registered as a therapeutic riding instructor). Melocco grew up as a 4-H kid in Ohio and now lives in view of Colorado's Rocky Mountains.

Sddita Fradette Blackburn

Acknowledgments

The writers wish to thank Amy Herdy, Cathy Laws and Rene Riley from Active Interest Media for their editing help. We would also like to thank our dear horse-riding friends, Suzi Carragher, Barbara Paciello, Sharon Cervantes, Amber Mathewson, Heather Browne, Shawntel Gallegos Wilson, Teri Kramer Mandel, Lucy Achenbach, Cheryl Lee and Sddita Fradette Blackburn, for adding great stories from the trail and for assisting with photos. And of course we thank the horses that have been our friends on the trail and our greatest teachers.

*Dedicated to all those who love
horses and want to be the best
for their equine friends.*

Contents

Introduction

MY TRAIL RIDING experience really began when I moved to Colorado in 1984. Prior to that, growing up in Florida, I rode my horse at high speed through rows of orange groves. We also had driving ponies that cruised back roads pulling our home-built stagecoach, which had a red coach and buck boards for those brave enough to ride shotgun. I also spent lots of time hanging out in the pasture with the horses—learning how they interacted and studying their every move. As a teenager, I spent my riding time in the English show arena—collecting ribbons and trophies, and learning the fine art of horsemanship.

My college years were spent in New Mexico at Thoroughbred breeding farms starting colts for the racetrack and riding at the racetrack. It satisfied my need for speed and I learned a lot about the horseracing side of the horse industry—with interesting lessons about horse training and human nature, too.

I had no plans to spend my life in the horse business. My parents intended for me to have a "real job." But when I left New Mexico and headed north (to find bigger mountains), the first job I was offered was guiding trail rides for tourists in the Rocky Mountains. Although the riders were ordinary tourists, these were not your everyday tourist rides—the terrain was steep and tough. I took riders who had never before been on horseback on long, arduous, and treacherous rides. Those riders had no clue how hazardous the trails were. We rode in the Sangre de Cristo Mountains—which are notoriously steep and not horse friendly—up to high mountain lakes above 12,000 feet above sea level, in terrain that would later become designated wilderness area. I also worked in the San Juan wilderness area, home to much more horse friendly but still high-mountain terrain. I packed in drop camps for campers and wrangled horses in full-service, guided hunts. I was even stranded for a few days above tree line in four feet of snow with 20 head of horses and mules to take care of. It was an exciting year, filled with one adventure after another. I gained a lot of good judgment from making a few mistakes.

The dude horses were incredible—you couldn't force them off the trail. They could pick their way through the craziest terrain as long as the riders were instructed to lay the reins down on the neck, hold on to the horn with both hands, and DO NOT MOVE! After riding fancy show horses and turbo-charged race horses valued at more than most people pay for a home, I learned to have the greatest respect for a good trail horse—especially one whose unfortunate lot in life is to pack around tourists riding in shorts and tennis shoes. A good trail horse is steady, sure footed, goes anywhere you point him, and does not look around, spook, or fuss with the other horses. Beyond being a good trail horse, a dude horse must be willing and able to pack around any rider, regardless of how out of balance he or she might be or how many conflicting signals the rider gives.

The first section of this book is dedicated to developing your skill as a rider, because I've

I'm riding Blue during an episode of "Horse Master" called "Close for Comfort."

seen how much the rider impacts the horse on the trail. Improving your horsemanship will help your horse so much! It will also make you more comfortable and confident out on the trail, whether you're off for a short excursion from your barn or on a major ride with others.

Within a year of moving to Colorado, I realized that I could make a living in the horse business—and I could turn a love for horses into a "real job." The next summer, I leased a string of dude horses and started my own business; the same business that I still operate today, although it has evolved through the years. Of course, those first dude horses are long gone, but I still make sure that every horse on my place is solid both in the arena and out on the trail. Throughout my trail-riding career—which, you'll understand, I like to say "ironically started as a job and then turned into a hobby"—I have had the great fortune of owning awesome guide

horses. A good dude horse is one thing, but a good guide horse is everything: one that will go anywhere you point him, alone or in company. I define a great guide horse as one that will forge any stream, open any gate, pony any horse, allow you to hop on and off without budging, and allow you to drop the reins and run to help a troubled rider. With that perfect trail partner, you can trust that your horse will be standing right where you left him without so much as flicking an ear.

Without question, my trail-riding experience has taught me that you have to be prepared for anything that can go wrong. You'll run into many interesting challenges if you ride long hours in the woods. Throughout my career, I have learned that people everywhere have the same horse problems and that horses everywhere have the same human problems; there is definitely a common thread among all horse people when it comes to problems. And this is why the second section of this book is about training and trouble-shooting problems with trail horses.

The truth is, trail riding is no different from any other riding discipline, whether you ride in circles, chase cows, jump crazy obstacles, or challenge the wilderness from the back of a horse, you need to be more than just a passenger and more than just a rider. You need to be a horseperson. For a safe, fun, and fulfilling trail-riding career, you need to:

- Ride your best (because at best, we stay out of our horse's way, and at worst, we impede his every step)

- Know how to manage your horse through any terrain

- Train your horse to be a great trail horse

- Deal with the common problems that occur with trail horses

I hope you will find many answers in this book and that it will inspire you to go beyond trail riding to trail horsemanship. At the end of each chapter, you'll find real-life questions and answers that relate to the topic of the chapter. You'll also find tips and tricks throughout the book that may come in handy down the road.

I also hope you enjoy this book and find plenty of information to keep you safe and happy as you ride. And if I am lucky, it will inspire you to become the best horseperson you can be, so that your horse will benefit, too!

Enjoy the ride,

Julie Goodnight

Julie Goodnight

Note to the reader: For simplicity's sake, and because my beloved horse Dually is a gelding, I refer to the horse as "him." For all of you with mares and fillies, there is no disrespect intended!

Julie's Lessons from the Trail

Dually and me.

EVERY DAY I SPEND WITH HORSES I learn something new and think of ideas and scenarios that teach me more about horsemanship—and how horsemanship applies to all we do in life. I hope you'll enjoy hearing about the lessons I've learned on the trail and the ideas I've pondered while riding and while prepping for long, leisurely rides. Before we get started with horsemanship how-to and training advice, take a moment to read a few lessons from my time on the trail . . .

Observation 1

Horses have taught me a lot in the past 50 years. There are three lessons I share often and make sure to repeat to myself:

- Never say never.
- Never say always.
- Plan for the worst-case scenario.

Horses will make a liar out of you. If you say that a particular horse is perfect and well-behaved, chances are he will embarrass you momentarily. If you take great pains to describe how bad your horse can be, he suddenly turns into a perfect angel. Have you ever had this experience with horses? I have, a bunch. Enough that I don't believe it's coincidence. Somehow horses know when you are bragging on them and they know when you're not and they have an uncanny ability to make a liar out of you. One of these days, I am going to figure out how they do that.

For example: Once, when showing a buyer a horse I had for sale—a mature and experienced trail horse—the buyer asked, "What does he do when he spooks?" My answer, in a moment of stupidity, was, "He never spooks." Of course, you can imagine what happened less than 15 minutes later. Note to self: NEVER say a horse never spooks. He was a good horse and I did sell him to that buyer, but now I know better than to say something like that.

One thing my father taught me about horses was to always keep the worst-case scenario in mind. For instance, I remember being on a pack trip with my father and we stopped for lunch at a high-mountain lake. He tied one of the horses to a huge dead tree trunk lying on the ground—this thing was at least two feet around—thinking it was surely an immovable object and therefore safe to use as an anchor. He was not keeping in mind the worst-case-scenario factor. Naturally, something startled the horse and he pulled back, moving the entire tree trunk and causing a much bigger spook. The wreck ended when something finally broke. If you keep in mind the worst that can happen and readjust your actions, you and your horse will be much safer.

Observation 2

One of the more intriguing comments I've eve

gotten came from a woman in one of my clinics. She didn't say much during the clinic—although it was obvious she was working hard and taking in as much information as possible. She was a good rider and had a nice horse and they seemed to be perfectly matched. Little did I know, until I received her note after the clinic, that she was a NASA astronaut and had piloted the space shuttle on four missions. What an accomplished woman! I can't say I was entirely surprised, because although she didn't say much during the clinic, she oozed competence and a quiet confidence—she was a kind and strong leader to her horse.

As usual, I spent a fair amount of time during the clinic talking about how crucial it is to control your horse's every action and to not let him get into the habit of making decisions on his own. This trait is critical in any environment and especially important on the trail. However, we humans have a habit of ignoring unauthorized actions of the horse—like letting him walk off without a cue when you mount or veering off the path you have dictated. We often rationalize our lack of leadership/authority by saying to ourselves, "Well, I was going to ask him to walk, anyway," or, "I was going to go that way, anyway." Although we may think it's a little thing, to the horse, his ability to take actions unauthorized by you is evidence of your lack of authority; and if *you* are not in charge, then *he* is.

The astronaut made some very astute observations on this subject in her email to me after the clinic. She said that a pilot must always be in control of her aircraft but that beyond control, when a pilot reaches a high level of competence it feels as though she is not working at control but rather that her aircraft is "strapped on" to her body and there is a sense of oneness. Again, I say, wow.

I've thought a lot about this idea and, ironically, when I got her email, I was in the midst of writing an article for a horse magazine about "wimpy" horse owners (the publisher's words, not mine) who refuse to take charge of their horses because they don't want to be "mean" to the horse but instead struggle and fight and fuss, constantly irritating and aggravating the horse, but never taking charge.

In reality, horses love and crave authority, structure and order, rules, and consequences. It makes them feel safe in the presence of a strong leader. Imagine if you were blasting off in the space shuttle. Wouldn't you want to believe your commander was strong, authoritative, unquestionably in control, and making all the decisions?

And I can't help but think of what it feels like to "strap your horse on." To me, this is the ultimate feeling on horseback—that you are one with your horse—and just thinking about it now makes me want to be on my horse and experience it again. Have you ever had the sheer joy of riding a horse that is so responsive to you that it feels as if *his* legs were *your* legs? That you have the power and athleticism yourself to jump big jumps, stop a fast-running cow or run like the wind? As corny as it sounds, being "one with the horse" is what we should all strive for.

"Strapping on" your horse goes way beyond just controlling your horse. First, you must show leadership to your horse so that he comes to respect you and look to you for direction. He must trust you implicitly and know that you always mean what you say, and that you will always be the commander; that you will always enforce the rules and treat your followers fairly, making him comfortable when he is compliant (release, release, release!) and issuing consequences when he is not. He must also know that you can be trusted to make good

decisions, and that through your leadership he will be safe, protected from confusion and fear, sure that he can do what you ask of him. These are tall orders.

If you reflect on your relationship with your horse, can you honestly say you are his commander? Or are you still grappling to control the aircraft? Does your horse want to blast off with you or is he looking for the nearest emergency exit? For the horse, every day on a new trail is like blasting off into space; his comfort and peace come from knowing there is someone in control of what could otherwise seem like a venture into chaos and confusion.

Observation 3

Whether in the arena or out on the trail, a horse's job is to go where you point him, on the path you dictate, at a speed you determine. The horse's focus should be on you and the task at hand, with little or no focus on the other horses, how far away the barn is, or what strangeness lurks around the corner. He must have a good work ethic—a get-the-job-done mentality, no matter what you ask, and a willingness to stand quietly and rest whenever the opportunity arises. He must be obedient and respect your authority and leadership without question. As I've said many times, there's really only one conversation to have with a horse and it goes like this: "Horse, this is your Captain speaking…."

Horses crave and search for authority—when there is structure and rules, they feel safe. It's a known fact of horse behavior that what motivates horses the most is comfort and security. And they feel safe and comfortable in the security of the herd. Unless and until you can give a horse the same sense of security and comfort he gets from the herd, he is not likely to want to go anywhere with you.

In every clinic I do, I see riders who lack true

authority over their horses. The horse walks off without a cue when the rider mounts, breaks into a trot when headed down a hill, breaks into a trot whenever he wants to, veers around or balks at challenging terrain, drags his toes when headed out, and gets in a hurry on the way back to the barn. Often the riders are in approximate control and have moments of authority over the horse, but it's a tenuous arrangement. The horse is constantly challenging the rider's authority and the rider is unwittingly condoning many small disobediences.

To a horse, you are either the leader all the time or you're not the leader. Horses are masters at recognizing leadership, authority, and consistency, and they will learn to disdain people who think they are the leader but aren't. That's why a horse will act one way with one rider and totally differently with another; and the reason why some horses get downright nasty when a person who lacks leadership tries to take control. Unfortunately, some horses learn that certain

"types" of people can be ignored and challenged, while others must be obeyed.

If a horse respects you as his leader, he will climb any mountain or cross any obstacle you ask him to. But you, as the leader, have a solemn responsibility to the horse to keep him safe and make him comfortable—by giving releases when they are due and letting him rest when he's earned it, and by keeping him safe and never asking anything of him that he is not capable of giving. You, as the leader, have the responsibility to define the rules and enforce them—making sure that compliance is rewarded and disobedience has ramifications. Your consistency and fairness are paramount.

I hope this book will guide you toward being a better leader to your horse, being the rider he deserves—keeping in balance with him and cueing him coherently with consistent and strong authority.

Julie Goodnight

SECTION 1

Trail Riding Skills

Perfect Posture:
Riding in a Balanced Position

How to Ride with Balance for a Secure and Comfortable Feel in the Saddle

Riding my friend's horse, Slide, I demonstrate proper position for trail riding.

"JUST TRAIL RIDING" IS A PHRASE I have chosen to delete from my vocabulary. Too often, I hear the phrase used to condone poor riding position or a lack of knowledge—"it doesn't matter; we're 'just' trail riding." Maybe at some point in the past, the idea of relaxing and just going for a simple ride through the fields sounded good to me—and easier than another equine pursuit. After working cattle all day or working on components of a reining pattern, maybe "just trail riding" sounded like a relaxing choice. Trail riding is a great addition to any horse's training and a great opportunity for horse and rider to bond. However, trail-ride time does not mean time to sit back in the chair position and be taken for a ride.

All who ride should consider themselves athletes, including those who trail ride, for there is no such thing as just trail riding. The phrase shouldn't allow you to know less about horses or riding techniques than any other rider. You must have great balance and ride actively in the proper position at all times along the trail. Your balance on the trail can be challenged at any point along the varying terrain. If your horse spooks at anything on the trail, your balance and position will keep you safe in the saddle.

One of our past "Horse Master" cast members, Shawntel Gallegos Wilson, once served as a trail guide in the Rocky Mountains. She rides her own horse bareback much of the time—to purposefully work on her balance. Shawntel says, "There's nothing to use as a crutch when you ride bareback—you're either balanced or you're off the horse." That balance has helped her on the trail when riding new horses just added to the trail string. Once, when a former "pasture ornament" was purchased for the dude string, he hadn't been ridden for years. It was Shawntel's job to get the horse ready for guests and ready for the trail. Shawntel was glad that her balance was good and her riding skills were well practiced. The horse had never been outside of an arena and spooked at every new scene. The problem was, he never spooked the same way twice; sometimes he bolted, sometimes he bucked, sometimes he turned in circles, and he even reared. Shawntel attributes her bareback riding skills for keeping her on that horse as she helped him learn to approach every scary scene with more and more confidence. "Only great balance can keep you on a horse like that—and save you from what could otherwise be a wreck," she says.

I rely heavily on my balance, position, and relaxation (yes, relaxation, even when the scenario doesn't seem relaxing at all) when training horses to approach new obstacles. On one of my favorite episodes of "Horse Master," I introduced a horse to the surf for the first time. On the show we called "Wave Runner," I had a wild ride as the

horse at first spooked, then decided to enter the ocean waves. Being able to stay in the middle of your saddle when the horse is moving dramatically is simply a matter of being relaxed and centered. I know, easier said than done. Anytime you tense a muscle, it causes you to lock a corresponding joint. Since your joints act as shock absorbers, a locked joint leads to bouncing. And if you lock your ankles, knees, or hips, it's the same as hitting the ejector button. The ride isn't

Perfect Posture

Horsemanship lesson: You'll learn how to avoid common position flaws, so you'll be safely balanced in the saddle, and so that you and your horse will feel better during and after your rides.

Why you need it on the trail: While you may love to relax and take in the scenery as you ride, it's important to actively ride and act as your horse's leader. As "the captain," you're in charge of where your horse goes and where he looks. A proper riding position will enable you to cue him effectively and let him know that you're not just a passenger along for a ride.

What you'll do: You'll feel the difference in your balance and position, and learn to correct yourself as soon as you're out of balance.

What you'll need: Your saddled horse, and a friend (or video camera) to help you identify and perfect your body alignment.

Skills your horse will need: Your horse should be responsive to your cues to move forward, stop, back, and side-to-side on your command. You'll need good steering and speed control at the walk and trot while riding in open spaces.

Position Fix 1: Create a Straight Line

comfortable for you or your horse if you're tense and unbalanced.

While I hope you don't have so much excitement and as many spooks out on the trail, working on your balance and learning to ride in an active, athletic position will help you be ready for anything that happens on the trail. Keep reading to find out how to ride actively in a balanced position and with relaxation.

Your position in the saddle affects your horse's ability to move freely. It also affects your safety, and how you'll feel during and after your ride.

If you sit back too far or brace in your stirrups, you'll risk aches and pains at the end of your ride. If you tense muscles and lock joints, not only do you expend a lot of muscle energy to stay on, but you'll bounce more in the saddle—jarring the joints of both you and your horse. You also won't be in the correct position to react and maintain your balance if your horse spooks or makes an unexpected step.

If your legs and feet aren't in the correct position, you may get uncomfortable on the ride and find it difficult to walk after you dismount.

Worse, you'll make your horse work harder than he would if you rode correctly.

In this chapter, I'll teach you how and why your ear, shoulder, hip, and heel alignment is important to your trail-riding position. I'll help you identify the common position flaws I see when trail riding. Then I'll help you correct—or avoid—such problems so you and your horse can hit the trails with comfort and balance.

Many trail riders complain about joint pain. Ankles, knees, hips, and back can stiffen and get sore, even on a smooth-gaited horse, if the rider's position is slightly off kilter. Slight adjustments in your alignment can help you ride smoothly and reduce the impact to both you and your horse.

Position Fix 1.
Create a Straight Line

As you ride, your legs should hang down from your hips in a position that would allow you to stand "on your own two feet" if your horse were not there to hold you up.

In Photo 1A, my legs are relaxed and hang-ing just behind my horse's cinch. You can draw a straight line through my ear, shoulder, hip, and heel. This line signals the correct position and shows that I'm balanced directly over my horse's center of gravity.

In Photo 1B, my lower leg is too far forward, and you can see my horse's cinch. This is called the "chair seat." It would take a jagged line to connect my ear, shoulder, hip, and heel, and this is an indication that the rider is out of balance.

This leg-forward position not only looks strange, but adversely affects your horse's performance. His center of gravity is located just behind his shoulder and below his withers. Ideally, you'll ride as close to that point as possible so that your weight is easy for him to carry, just as it would be if you were carrying someone piggy-back.

When you're balanced and sitting above your heels, you're as close to this balance point as possible. When your legs slide forward, your weight shifts back and drives down into your horse's back and loins.

Your horse feels this uncomfortable balance shift just as you would if someone you carried on your back suddenly shifted back and pointed her feet toward your shoulders. The weight would become difficult to carry.

To find this optimum leg position and whole-body alignment, place your reins in one hand, hold your saddle's horn or pommel with your free hand, roll up onto your thighs as you stand up in the stirrups and find the balanced position; keep your knees bent and notice where your stirrups and legs are positioned. Also see whether you can easily balance without holding on to the horn. If you let go of the horn and fall back into the saddle, your legs were too far forward. To maintain the balanced alignment when you stand, your lower leg will move way back as you stretch your heel down. Make sure

you aren't pushing up off the stirrup and stiffening your knees, but rather using your thighs to lift and open your hips.

When you can balance easily (it may take some practice), roll back onto your seat bones, sit up straight, and allow your legs to relax against your horse's sides. Your legs should be back underneath you now.

If this position feels new and strange, ask a friend to watch you ride. Ask her to tell you when you have a perfect vertical line between your heel, hip, shoulder, and ear, and when your leg begins to drift forward and out of balance.

Sometimes, saddle design can contribute to a chair-seat position. For instance, if the stirrups hang in front of the seat's center, the saddle will draw your legs forward. If your stirrups are too long as they might be in an effort to reduce joint pain (see page 11, "Angle Your Ankles," for a better way to alleviate joint pain), it's difficult to keep your leg underneath you.

Pushing your heels down too far and leaning back on the cantle can also cause you to brace and push your legs forward and out of alignment. You may actually be pushing your legs too far forward by trying to put your heels down too much or because you are nervous on your horse. Usually, just relaxing your leg entirely will help it hang straight down. Also, in a Western saddle, stiffening and bracing your legs may cause the stirrup leathers to slide forward on the bars of the tree. So you may need to shimmy the leathers back into place to help with your leg position.

Position Fix 2.
Nix the Splits

In a relaxed and correct position, your lower leg hangs down from your knee and wraps around your horse's barrel, softly caressing your horse's

Position Fix 2: Nix the Splits

sides (Photo 2A). Note that you can't see much daylight between my leg and the horse's side.

If your legs are too straight and you're riding in "splits" position (Photo 2B), it's time to relax and sit down on your seat bones. Riding with your legs far from your horse's sides pushes you up out of the saddle, and off your seat bones. Your whole body becomes tense, and you lose the ability to signal your horse with subtle seat and leg cues.

You may also tense your whole spine, which can cause your horse's gaits to pound your spine and tense your shoulders. Instead, allow your body to relax and go with your horse's rhythmic flow. Any muscle that you tense, whether it's in your shoulders, your back, your arms, your legs, or your rear end, causes a corresponding joint to lock up. Your joints—especially your

ankles, knees, and hips—are your major shock absorbers and these joints constantly open and close to absorb the movement and rhythm in your horse's back. Tensing your muscles leads to bouncing.

And, while it's good to ride with your heel below your toe so that your foot stays in the stirrup and your weight is sinking down, it's not necessary to press your legs down and out. Doing so will cause your joints to lock, which leads to bouncing and can cause ankle and knee pain.

To find this optimum leg position, bend your knees, relax your legs, and think of your stirrups more as a foot rest and not something to push on. Keep your heel lower than your toe, but don't push on the stirrup. Ask a friend to stand in front of you as you walk straight ahead, and

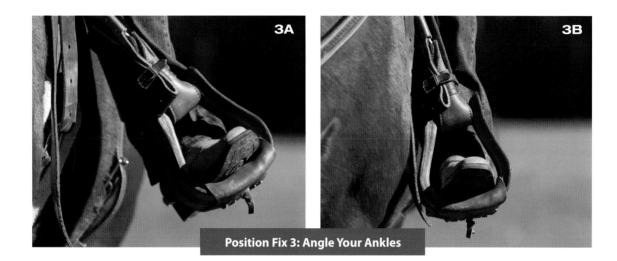

Position Fix 3: Angle Your Ankles

also to the side to check your alignment and alert you when you stiffen your legs or your legs are too far forward.

Position Fix 3.
Angle Your Ankles

Flex your toes and point them out just a little so that your foot is equally weighted in the stirrup across the balls of your feet. This slightly angled position (Photo 3A), called pronating, simply means to roll your ankle inward so that the weight is balanced evenly across the ball of your foot and your joints are in alignment.

This is the key to joint comfort when you ride for long distances. The pronated position of your foot will realign the bones that comprise your ankle and knee joints as you ride—and can reduce joint pain.

I remember being told as a child to keep my toes pointed straight ahead as I rode. Yet you don't walk with your feet pointed straight forward; if you try, you'll find it's difficult to maintain your balance. Also, your hips and knees don't move as fluidly as they should when your feet are parallel.

When you ride with your toes pointing

straight ahead (Photo 3B), a position riding instructors used to drill as "proper"—you actually cause great stress on your joints. When you sit on a horse, your legs are spread unnaturally apart, putting stress on the ankle, knee, and hip joints in the classic bow-legged position, with crooked joints. When you pronate your ankle, it realigns the bones that comprise those joints and helps alleviate joint stress and pain. By relaxing and flexing your foot and following the stirrup angle so that the sole of your boot turns outward, you'll feel more relaxed, both on and off your horse.

Position Fix 4.
Arch No More

Keep your back relaxed, but straight (Photo 4A). If you concentrate too hard on your position and posture, it's easy to overcompensate, stiffen your back muscles and ride incorrectly (Photo 4B).

I often see riders arch their backs when I ask them to sit up straight. The position causes tension in your back muscles and forces a curve into your spine, making you sit too far forward and off your seat bones. It can quickly become tiring, and is painful for both you and your horse if you trot. In this position, you'll slam down onto your horse's back and land on your crotch instead of your seat bones.

If you get nervous during your ride, or if your horse makes a sudden move and becomes difficult to control, it's easy for your reflexes to kick in and move you into a perched position. With an arched back, your weight will shift forward, your heels will lift, and your hands will clench the reins, causing many problems for both you and your horse.

This tense position transmits inadvertent signals to your horse, telling him to tense (or tense more), speed up, and possibly prepare for flight. This position also causes you to close your pelvis, which reduces your hips' range of motion and leads to bouncing in the saddle.

If you often ride with tension, this perched-forward position can cause soreness in your knees, hips, and seat, as well as to your horse's back.

Instead, soften your back, suck your belly button toward your spine, and relax your lower back just as you do when you sit back into a car seat or easy chair. This is an open pelvis: When you have all your weight on your two seat bones (not on your crotch), your lower back is flat, opening the angle between your hips and thighs. When your back is flat and relaxed, you'll feel your hips swinging with your horse's back as he moves in his rhythmic gait.

The rougher your horse's gait, the more important it is that your back and legs are relaxed and that your pelvis is open. When your legs are relaxed, you'll also be able to relax your hips, so they can absorb the spring in your horse's stride.

Position Fix 4: Arch No More

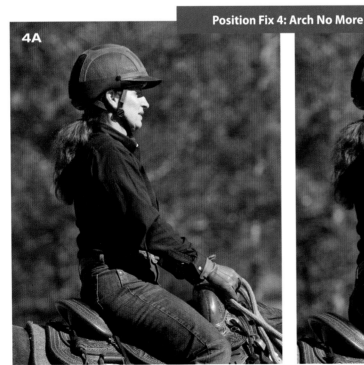

4A

4B

Q&A
WITH JULIE

Using Natural Aids

Question: How do you teach riders to use all the natural aids together—leg and rein aids?

Answer: The natural aids are the best tools the rider has to communicate with the horse. Traditionally, there are four natural aids: the seat (weight), the legs, the hands, and the voice of the rider. I prefer to teach seven natural aids, which—in addition to the traditional four aids—includes the rider's eyes, the rider's breathing, and the rider's brain. When all of these aids are used together, it gives a clear and consistent communication to the horse of what you want him to do, and sets your body up to naturally give the correct cue. All of the natural aids should be used in unison and should always originate, or be connected to, the use of the seat. No one aid gives a cue to the horse (you do not stop by pulling on the reins or go by kicking), but all the aids working together will guide the horse toward the appropriate response.

For instance, asking the horse to stop or slow down is not simply a matter of pulling back on the reins. To ask the horse to stop using all of the aids in a connected fashion, first the rider must drop her weight onto the horse's back by opening and relaxing the pelvis and plugging her seat bones into the saddle. As the seat of the rider drops down on the horse's back, a connection is made between the rider's elbows and hips. The shift of the rider's weight and opening of the rider's pelvis will cause an increase of the pressure on the horse's mouth through the rider's arms, hands, and reins. In other words, the pressure the horse feels on his mouth is connected to the increased weight on his back, and the pull comes from the rider's entire body and weight, not just from the hands.

You can see how this feels by sitting in a chair pulled up to a table. With both feet flat on the floor and sitting up straight, put both hands on the edge of the table. As you exhale and rotate the seat bones forward and down (opening the pelvis and plugging the seat bones into the chair), pull on the edge of the table so that your seat bones get even heavier on the chair. This is how you cue the horse for a stop or to slow down by using your weight aid first. You should feel a connection from your arms to your seat bones as they press into the chair. If your seat bones lighten, and your upper body moves forward when you pull back on the reins, your aids are not connected. Practice this exercise until you feel the connection between your seat and hands, and then try to feel the connection on a horse.

To use all of the aids in a connected fashion to ask the horse to turn, the rider must first look in the direction of the turn and use her eyes and torso to initiate the turn. As the rider's head turns slightly in the direction of the turn, the shoulders will follow, swiveling slightly in the saddle and shifting the rider's weight to her outside seat bone. Again, the legs and hands will follow the movement of the rider's seat and not act independently. The outside leg will sink down and close on the horse's side, shutting the door to the outside. Conversely, the rider's inside leg will lift up slightly as the inside seat bone lightens, opening the door to the inside and keeping the horse's inside shoulder elevated in an arcing turn. As the seat swivels slightly on the horse's back, the elbows, arms, and shoulders of the rider will follow (make sure your upper arms are in contact with your rib cage), giving a release with the outside rein and increased pressure to the inside rein, thus supporting the horse's head, neck, and shoulders in the turn.

Using your whole body and having all of the aids give the same signal is a very effective way to communicate with the horse and results in invisible cues and seamless transitions.

For more answers, visit the Training Library: www. juliegoodnight. com/ traininglibrary

Over the Hill:
Find Your Balance on Steep Terrain

Gracie and I prepare to ride through the hilly terrain around the C Lazy U Ranch in Granby, Colorado.

YOUR POSITION IN THE SADDLE IS important on the flat, but it's even more important when you're riding over steep terrain. I often receive emails from trail riders reporting scary—and sometimes even humorous—tales about accidents on hills. I've noticed that most of the stories fit into two categories: (1) accidents that happen because of riding with groups who aren't considerate and speed up on hills, or (2) accidents that happen because of rider position.

One "Horse Master" show fan, Teri Mandel from northeast Nebraska, wrote in to report an incident that she says stopped her from wanting to ride with large groups. As the group with whom she was riding approached a ravine, riders at the front of the herd decided it would be fun to have a "Man From Snowy River" moment, so they broke into a gallop as they headed downhill. Though she didn't want to move into a speedy gait, her horse's herd mentality kicked in and it was tough to keep him from joining the fast action. With the huge group thundering downhill, one rider fell off his horse and into a creek as others galloped around him. "I still can't believe the rider wasn't trampled by the other horses," Teri wrote. "I'm a firm believer in letting my horse find his own path if the terrain is tough, and I just can't imagine wanting to go fast and not carefully pick my path."

Lesson learned: If you're riding with others, make sure you know all members of the group well and share an agreed-upon trail etiquette. No one should speed up without alerting the whole group and making sure that all agree that it's time for a pace change—especially if you're riding up and down hills. And a speed change on an incline is usually not a good idea.

Keep in mind that if your horse is totally obedient, he would not break gait or change speed without a direct order from you to do so. But so often I see horses that break into a trot whenever they want, or walk off without a cue because the horse in front of them started walking, or walk off as soon as the rider's rear end hits the saddle. If the horse is changing speed without a cue from the rider, the horse is disobedient and he should be corrected (with a harsh stop in the case of a horse speeding up or a spank of the reins if he slows down unauthorized). Often, the rider stays passive at this point. Unfortunately, being passive sends a message to your horse that you condone his disobedience, so he will most certainly do it again and again. Once you start letting your horse make decisions, it won't be long until he makes a decision you do not agree with.

Riding alone may not pose the risk of galloping with the masses, but if you don't consider your riding position, you just may find yourself hung up and in an embarrassing situation (though slightly humorous if all is corrected quickly). Another friend—who will remain anonymous—admits that she's leaned too far forward and caught the elastic of her bra over the horn "more times than anyone should admit." Being out of position can also pose dangerous and difficult-to-correct outcomes.

I know of a rider who pulled back on the reins and moved her body weight too far back as her horse spooked on a hilly trail. The resulting flip was fun for no one—the horse fell onto the rider as the two struggled to regain their balance. But enough of these fear-inducing stories; read on to find out how you should position yourself to ride the hills without a problem. If you stay centered on your horse, you'll be just fine.

Do you dread seeing a steep hill on the trail? Do you worry that your horse will speed up, lunging out of control or

Over the Hill

Horsemanship lesson: You'll learn how to position your body so that your horse can carry you easily on hills. You'll also learn how to keep your horse's attention on you and to stop him from speeding up on his own.

Why you need it on the trail: Hills are a part of most every trail. You may also trailer your horse to mountainous areas where slopes can be steep and treacherous. It's important to navigate the climbs and descents so that you and your horse are balanced, and can move safely and easily. It's also important to make sure your horse listens to your cues for speed—even if he's tired or wants to gain momentum.

What you'll do: You'll learn to ride in a balanced position and learn how your horse's balance changes according to a hill's steepness. You'll also learn how to identify your horse's minor disobediences so that you remain confident and in control.

What you'll need: Your horse tacked up with his usual saddle. On steep terrain, add a breast collar and crupper or britchin, if needed. You'll also need a hill or slope on which to practice.

Skills your horse will need: Your horse should be responsive to your cues to move forward, stop, back, and side-to-side. You should have good steering and speed control at the walk and trot while riding in open spaces.

Step 1: Refine Your Hill-Riding Position

charging down the hills in a ground-pounding trot without brakes? Do you feel like you aren't secure in the saddle as the ground slopes beneath you?

If you don't feel secure in the saddle and trust that your horse will listen to your speed cues, any slight change in altitude turns into a challenge, especially as you ride up and down rocky or slippery, muddy hills.

Here, I'll teach you how to sit securely as you ride up and down hills. I'll also help you gain control of your horse's speed, no matter what the terrain. First, I'll help you position your body so that you help your horse climb up and down hills safely and in balance.

Then, I'll help you note and correct common hill-induced bad behaviors, so you stay in control of your horse's speed and direction.

I often see riders lean forward or back too much as they're riding up and down hills (or fail to adjust at all to the horse's change of balance). It's common for riders to think that you should lean far forward as you ride uphill or far back

as you ride downhill. But those positions can actually make it more difficult for your horse to carry you. It's important to stay centered over your horse's center of gravity and ride so that you help your horse carry you and him up and down hills easily. Remember that your center of gravity should be aligned with the horse's balance point.

I also see riders who allow their horses to make small but meaningful (if you're a horse) decisions about where to place their feet or how fast to go. While it's sometimes important to allow your horse to navigate and choose his own foot placement (on your signal), it's never acceptable to allow him to choose his own speed on hills.

If your horse chooses his own speed as he goes up and down hills—such as lunging up the hills or trotting down them—you're teaching him that he doesn't need to listen to you and that he's in charge. That's setting you up to have a disobedient horse in many situations—not just when it comes to riding on hills.

Step 1.
Refine Your Hill-Riding Position

You've probably heard that you should lean forward as you head uphill and lean back as you ride down. While that teaching isn't wrong, it's overly simplistic. It's important to refine your position to help your horse stay balanced on hills.

You actually need to stay in an upright position as the level of your horse's back changes with the hill's slope. Imagine a tree trunk growing on the side of a steep hill. The tree trunk doesn't lean; it grows perpendicularly from the horizon, straight to the sky, even though the slope of the ground changes.

Similarly, as you ride your horse up and down hills, your torso should remain vertical and match the tree trunks. With this position, you'll stay upright and centered on your horse. It will be much easier for the horse to balance you when your center of gravity is balanced over his.

When you ride on flat ground and strive for a balanced position, you keep a straight line through your ear, shoulder, hip, and heel. On the flat, this line is vertical (or perpendicular to the ground).

When you ride up a hill, keep this perfect-posture alignment, but change your placement in the saddle. Keep the line from your ear to heel perpendicular to the horizon instead of matching your alignment to your saddle's tilted position.

As you ride up a hill, position yourself so that the line from your ear to heel cants forward. Move your lower leg slightly back, and move your head and shoulders slightly forward; move as little or as much as needed to match the steepness of the hill while maintaining the straight line and keeping your balance.

Don't sit with your leg too far forward, which

will cause your seat to rest against the cantle in a chair-sitting position. Although this position may be comfortable for you, you're not in balance with your horse and the broken line in your ear-shoulder-hip-heel alignment may cause your horse to work harder to carry your unbalanced body.

In Photo 1A, my lower legs are back and my upper body is canted forward. If I wasn't riding and instead was walking uphill, my body would be in the same canted-forward position, and I could maintain my balance as I hiked up.

Whether going up or down, you may need to lift the weight off your seat bones, as I am here, so that your horse can round his back and bring his hind end up underneath him. Don't lean forward or back, but stay upright, and just transfer the weight from your seat bones to your thighs and stirrups.

As you ride up steeper terrain, it's a good idea to reach far forward to grasp your horse's mane, as your body is already tilted forward. It will actually help him pull your weight up the hill and help you keep your weight centered. Getting "left behind" when your horse lunges up a steep embankment is really hard on your horse.

When you ride downhill, your ear-to-heel alignment will shift so that your lower leg is in front of your head—all the while matching the lines of the trees. In Photo 1B, my position matches the tree to the left of my shoulder. I'm riding in a position that's perpendicular to the horizon and matches the trees.

When you ride downhill and behind the vertical, your lower leg comes slightly forward as your shoulders move back. But if you lean too far back and push too much weight in the stirrups, it may cause your saddle to slip forward, causing shoulder soreness and girth sores, and affecting your horse's balance.

2A

Step 2: Control Your Speed

I realize that many riders fear going downhill. Concentrating on your heel and ankle position can help you feel safe and in control. Keep weight in your heels and pronate your ankles by angling your foot and placing more weight on your big toe (Photo 1B). By pronating your ankles when you're in tricky terrain, you'll gain security and bring your lower legs close to your horse's sides, helping you stay centered on his center of gravity.

Step 2.
Control Your Speed

Many riders allow their horses to speed up on hills and the horses learn that their disobedience (changing speed without a cue) is allowed on steep terrain. Often, this is compounded by the rider taking a death-grip on the horn with both hands and failing to take control of the horse with the reins. Making sure you're in charge of the speed will help you feel secure on the slopes and remind your horse that you're the leader.

Horses often start up a hill at a walk, then lunge into a trot or lope to pull themselves up—getting their momentum up is easier than pulling the rider's weight steadily up the hill. As they lurch up the hill, riders feel out of control and unsure of how to balance. On descents, horses may start at a walk, then trot down when gravity and momentum kick in.

It's sometimes difficult for your horse to collect himself and maintain the walk as he moves up and down hills, and it's easier to lurch forward. However, his compliance with your chosen gait is possible, even though it requires more effort on his part. If he doesn't comply, he may be acting lazy or downright disobedient.

A gait change can also cause problems if you're riding with a group. It's poor trail etiquette to change to a fast gait without alerting your riding buddies so that they can make the necessary adjustments. Trail riders with good etiquette and awareness of the group will actually slow down to close ranks when approaching an incline or other challenging terrain, so that all the horses move along steadily; and they'll make sure that all horses in the group are through the obstacle before speeding up.

Anytime your horse changes gait without a cue, he's making an unauthorized decision and therefore being disobedient. You may occasionally ask for a trot or lope as you ride up a shallow hill for conditioning or training purposes, but that decision should be yours and not initiated by your horse. If you do decide to trot or lope

your horse on hills, you should cue up the horse before the hill and make sure the horse maintains a steady rhythm as he goes up or down.

If you allow your horse to make one unauthorized decision, he'll begin making others, and sooner or later, he'll make a decision that you don't like.

If your horse has learned the bad habit of speeding up on hills, you'll have to check his speed by stopping along the way. Use your voice, seat, and rein aids in sequential order to help your horse understand you want to stop or slow down.

To reinforce your "whoa" command, shift your weight back and pull up and back on the reins. If you need to slow your horse as you head down, sit back with your weight/seat, and then pick up on the reins. It often helps to halt at the top of the hill before proceeding down. Then check your horse's speed as you descend by asking him to halt every few steps.

In Photo 2A, my hands are positioned in front of my saddle's pommel in preparation to cue my horse to slow down with a *half-halt* (a

Tack for Steep Terrain

You'll need the following:

Breast collar: This goes around the chest of the horse and attaches to the saddle, either at the D-rings or higher, to prevent the saddle from sliding too far back on steep uphill grades. For trail riding, it's best to have a collar that attaches high on the saddle and/or with a strap over the neck in front of the withers to prevent interference with the horse's shoulders.

Crupper: attaches to a D-ring at the very back/center of the saddle and loops under the tail to prevent the saddle from slipping forward on steep downhill grades. Cruppers are specially made to be easy to get under the tail and smooth and comfortable for the horse. The horse must be accustomed to having his tail handled and desensitized to having the crupper strap under his tail.

Britchin: a long, wide strap that goes around the rear end of the horse and attaches at the flank cinch D-rings of the saddle. It hangs from smaller straps over the horse's rump and prevents the saddle from slipping forward on steep downhill grades. Saddles must be rigged to accommodate a britchin and it must be sized for the horse. A britchin is especially useful for mules.

3A

Step 3: Pick a Safe Path

momentary application of seat and rein aids and sometimes with leg aids, too). I'm also sitting securely on my seat bones, so I can cue my horse to slow with my seat aids at the same time.

Tip: Don't allow too much distance between horses if you're riding with a group. If the line is too spread out, your horse may trot to catch up—especially on hills. You should be able to see the hind feet of the horse in front of you between your horse's ears. As the lead rider, you'll want to stop at the top of a steep descent to gather up the herd and proceed slowly down one after the other in tighter formation.

Step 3.
Pick a Safe Path

Although you usually want to control your horse's speed and direction, there are times when it's appropriate to allow your horse to choose his steps so that he can find the safest way through rocks or timber or tricky water crossings. In self-preservation mode, most horses will pick the best route and find it easier to balance the load without interference from the reins. In very steep and rugged terrain—and especially when it's rocky—give your horse control of his head so that he can balance and pick his way. But keep in mind that he has no way of judging the clearance over his head and if allowed to choose his path, he may go under a low-lying branch that you cannot duck under, so some supervision may be necessary.

Your horse needs the freedom of his head to balance. Although you should use your reins (in coordination with your weight/seat cues), if your horse speeds up on hills, holding excessive contact on the horse's mouth can impair his balance and cause him to slip or fall. Reach forward as you head up hills and don't "ride the brakes" as you descend.

When you reach forward and loosen the reins (Photo 3A), your horse will know that it's okay to control his own head and pick his route through difficult terrain. In these instances, you'll usually be on an obvious trail, which he knows he should follow.

If your horse veers off a trail immediately and tries to turn back toward home, he may not be reliable and well-trained enough to be riding in rugged terrain. Go back to easier terrain and do more basic training, paying close attention to your horse's obedience.

Upper Body Position

Question: How should my upper body be as I ride?

Answer: Much focus is given to the rider's seat and leg position, as it should be, for these are critical areas that affect equitation. However, the upper body (head, neck, chest, shoulders, and arms) should not be forgotten, and constant attention must be given to these body parts, as well, to develop effective riding skills.

Remembering the all-important balanced riding position of ear-shoulder-hip-heel alignment, you might say that half of your balance comes from upper body position. And for the horse, nothing is more important than correct arm and hand position, which in turn leads to soft and clear communication from the rider's hands to the horse's mouth. Starting at the top and working our way down, we must first con-sider head and neck position. The most common equitation mistakes in this area are eyes looking down and the rider's chin jutting forward with the ear stretching in front of her shoulder in a position I fondly refer to as "the Cro-Magnon look."

Your eyes are an important means of communication with your horse, not to mention a critical tool for balance (look forward and you'll go forward; look down and you'll go down). Your horse is naturally programmed to look and go where the herd leader (alpha individual) looks and goes. This is an important survival tool and ingrained herd behavior. If you have developed the kind of relationship that you should with your horse, he should consider you to be his leader and will be tuned into your eyes and where you look, so it's important to keep that line of communication open. Keeping your eyes focused ahead will also help increase your personal level of confidence as well.

As for balance, our heads are pretty large and heavy so any fraction of an inch out of the balance position (you are balanced when your ears are over your shoulders) will throw your balance off con-siderably. If you struggle with ear alignment, think of keeping your nose behind your belt buckle or touching the back of your neck to your shirt collar.

Shoulders are another com-mon area for equitation faults, but often the root of the problem of rounded shoulders is overlooked. An

You shouldn't have to micromanage your trail horse. Like any obedient horse, he should go straight on the path you indicate, without constant guidance. The more rugged the terrain, the more important it is that he have freedom of his head to balance.

Surefooted horses will do a great job at picking their own routes. But not all horses are naturally surefooted. If your horse is a klutz, practice on obstacles and ground poles at home. This will help him to pay more attention to where he puts his feet on the trail.

If your horse habitually speeds up going downhill, or you feel that he's not picking a safe path, it may help to follow a well-trained horse that takes the hills slowly and methodically. You'll gain confidence and will get into a balanced position more easily when you can trust the horse beneath you.

Upper Body Position *(continued)*

old-fashioned style of teaching is to ask riders to "put their shoulders back" in an effort to keep the rider more upright and to fix poor posture. I find that the rider with rounded shoulders does not really have a shoulder problem at all but is instead usually collapsing the rib cage onto her spine. The solution does not lie in stiffening the shoulders, which forces them back, but rather in lifting the sternum (breast bone), lifting the rib cage, and lengthening the spine.

If rounded shoulders and poor upper body posture are a problem for you, try lifting your sternum toward the sky or inflating your lungs fully and keeping your collar bones lifted as you exhale. Remember, poor posture in the saddle probably started with poor posture on the ground, so work on these issues when you are not riding, too.

Arm and hand position can be all over the map, instead of in the neat and tidy "box" of proper position. Imagine a six-inch square right in front of the saddle horn—that's where your hands should stay. Upper arms should stay close to your body, with your shoulders hanging straight down. The line from your neck to your arms should be long and relaxed, with your hands in front of the saddle and stretching for your horse's mouth. Elbows need to stay bent and will open and close to act as shock absorbers as your horse moves, allowing you to maintain a steady amount of contact with the horse's mouth. Any pulling action on the reins should come from your elbows, pulling your hands toward your hips, not pulling down or up on the reins. Your upper arms and elbows should always be connected to your rib cage and your arms should move with your rib cage and body, not independently.

There should always be an imaginary straight line from your elbow to the horse's mouth. Try to visualize this line as you ride and realize that your hand position will change as the horse's head changes in elevation. A common problem in beginner riders is hands held too high, and a common fault of more experienced riders is to keep their hands too low. Remember your six-inch square box in front of the pommel of your saddle and try to keep your hands always "in the box."

Another common problem seen in hand position is broken wrists or flat "piano hands." The straight line from elbow to mouth can be broken in many ways through the wrists. Wrists should always remain straight with the hands angled slightly inward, just as if you were reaching out to shake someone's hand. Hands must not be too close together or too far apart because this too can break your straight line from elbow to horse's mouth.

Straight lines are an important component of proper riding position, whether it's the straight line of ear-shoulder-hip-heel alignment, a straight head and neck, a straight spine (flat back), or the line from your elbow to the horse's mouth. A straight line is always the shortest distance between two points and the strongest, most balanced, and most effective line of communication with your horse.

For more answers, visit the Training Library: www. juliegoodnight. com/ traininglibrary

Emergency Brake:
Learn to Stop Any Horse

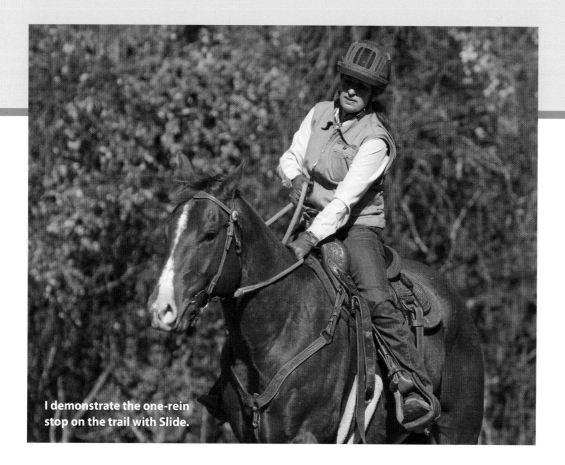

I demonstrate the one-rein stop on the trail with Slide.

O
NE OF MY "HORSE MASTER" TELEVISION SHOWS from our second year featured a lesson on how to perform the pulley rein stop. It's an emergency stop technique that isn't taught as often as the one-rein stop, but it does have its time and place. If you're on the trail and can't turn your horse because of steep terrain or gnarly brush, the pulley rein will help you stop on a dime while staying on a straight course. The day after this particular show aired, I received this email from a horsewoman in Southern California named Suzi—who has since become a friend and companion at my West Coast shows. She learned the skill one day and used it the very next.

"I was asked to look after my friend's Thoroughbred gelding for the weekend," reports Suzi. "He was a great horse! Easygoing and gentle, but had his vices—one of which was shying away from things that "appeared." So part of my routine was to use the trail as a reward for good arena work. It wasn't a very difficult trail, heck, it was downright easy, but it wasn't an arena.

So off we went. Everything was going well, and then I saw them: two longhorn cattle munching happily on brush right on the fence line where we needed to go. There wasn't a way around them. So I had a decision to make: Do we turn around and go back or do we proceed as if nothing was out of the ordinary? I chose the latter.

"I asked him to go forward. He did. And then I felt his body change underneath me. He was still walking, so I acted like this is a normal, everyday thing that horses do and live to tell others about it. Just as we passed the longhorns, one of them shook its head, making lots of noise in the brush. That did it. The horse balled up and bolted down the trail. It's amazing how MUCH data goes through your head in a short period of time.

"My initial thought was, 'Do I try to get this under control and act like it was my idea to move out, or do I stop this train?' Then, I thought, 'You know, with my luck we'll run into a rabbit hole and then we're both dead, so I better stop. How do I stop again?' I tried the normal everyday cue and he blew right through it. 'There's gotta be something else I can do,' I thought, then remembered what Julie had just shown on TV—THE PULLEY REIN! I shortened one rein, set my hand on his withers and pulled up on the opposite rein. I remember saying out loud to myself, the horse, the birds, and that @#$%^ longhorn, 'Holy cow, it worked!' "

I'm so glad the technique was in Suzi's bag of tools to use when she needed it, and that she had the wherewithal to remember how to execute the pulley rein without having practiced it. Practicing the technique can be hard on your horse and shouldn't be done often, but it's good to go through the motions—even off of your horse—just to know what to do in case you need it in a dire emergency. I hope you never have to use it, but here's what to do.

If you don't know how to stop in an emergency, riding can be a nerve-wracking sport. You wouldn't drive a car that didn't have

Emergency Brake

Horsemanship lesson: You'll learn how to stop in an emergency, practicing the procedure before you need it.

Why you need it on the trail: When riding in an uncontrolled environment, you never know when something may jump out and startle your horse. A situation on the trail may trigger your horse's flight response. Some horses spook in place, some may spin around, and some aren't bothered at all—but some horses may bolt. Any horse is capable of spooking and bolting at any time. To avoid a potential disaster, you need to plan for the worst-case scenario by keeping one hand on the reins at all times and by knowing how to execute an emergency stop.

What you'll do: You'll learn to stop your horse in two ways. First, you'll learn the one-rein stop—handy when your horse becomes excited or tense. Then you'll learn the pulley-rein stop to use if he gets out of control.

What you'll need: Your saddled horse and 9- or 10-foot, single-loop rope reins that are easy to collect and handle. In this lesson's photos I am using using reins I designed to be easy to shorten and lengthen; they are nine feet long, measured end-to-end, and the perfect length for trail riding on an average to large horse (for a really long and tall horse, you may want 10-foot reins).

Skills your horse will need: Your horse should accept a rider, and respond to a voice and rein cue to whoa.

brakes! When you ride, you need to know that you can stop the horse under any circumstances, since flight is the strongest instinctive behavior of horses and since even the most trusted trail horses may occasionally have reason to spook and bolt.

In this chapter, I'll teach you how to stop your horse in practice sessions so that you'll know what to do in an emergency. Inevitably, there are spooks and startles out on the trail. When your horse's flight instinct is triggered, your ride can go from mild to wild in a heartbeat.

To ease your worries and ensure you have a braking system, I'll show you the one-rein stop for use when your horse gets a little strong or emotional. I'll also teach the "if-all-else-fails" pulley-rein stop to use if your horse bolts or runs away with you, or is totally out of control.

Whenever you ask for a stop, use your seat aids first. Otherwise, you teach your horse that you'll pull on his mouth constantly, wearing out the brake pads. Teach him to stop with your seat cues, without any rein aids at all. Think of your reins not as a cue, but as reinforcement—a backup plan—if your horse fails to listen to your seat cue.

In my everyday riding, I teach my horses to stop when I exhale and say "whoa." Then I shift my weight back. I pick up the reins only as a last resort (as reinforcement to the seat cue) and if I have to pick them up, I do so in a meaningful way—applying enough pressure to abruptly stop and to make the horse think a little harder next time I use my seat cue. No horse in the world wants his mouth pulled on, and he's usually happy to stop, so if he gets a cue before the rein contact, he'll usually obey.

Step 1.
Teach the One-Rein Stop

If you pull on two reins at the same time to stop your horse, the pressure on his mouth will be so great that he'll lean into the pressure and brace against it. The pressure from two reins hurts. The result is a horse that pulls the reins out of your hands and doesn't listen to your stop cue, a behavior known as "running through the bridle."

A horse stopped with two reins' worth of pressure at once (even with a snaffle bit in place) learns to pull, travel with his head held high, and hollow his back. He'll often develop

Step 1: Teach the One-Rein Stop

1A

1B

strong muscles on his neck's underside. Using the correct bit for your horse's level of training and the type of riding you do can make a huge difference to your horse. For more information on the best bit to use for your horse, visit www.juliegoodnight.com/myler.

What's worse, I often see riders who pull constantly with more and more pressure when a horse doesn't stop right away. A horse's natural reaction to pain and discomfort is to run away from it. A horse can learn to speed up instead of slow down when the rider thinks she's telling him to stop. The result is a battle of constant pulling.

You won't win this tug of war with your horse. His weight will allow him to win, and he won't listen to your two-handed stop cue because his mind shuts down as soon as he starts bracing and pulling.

The good news is that it's easy to teach your horse not to force against your rein aids by teaching him to give to one hand and one side—this is called the one-rein stop.

When you want to slow down or stop your horse without a brace in his response, simply shorten one rein, then lift that rein up and back, bringing your hand toward your belly button (Photo 1A). At the same time, shift your weight back in the saddle and say, "whoa," if you intend to fully stop.

Your sequence of cues will turn your horse's head to the side and cause his hip to disengage from forward impulsion. Simply put, he'll cross his back legs and lose his forward momentum (Photo 1B).

Disengaging the hindquarters not only stops your horse's speed and helps him listen to you, but also puts him in a submissive state of mind. When you perform this maneuver, ask a friend to watch your horse's movements from the ground to make sure he's crossing his legs, with the inside hind leg crossing in front. You should be able to feel this disengagement very clearly from the saddle as his back becomes distinctly crooked.

To make sure your horse knows to stop (not just turn) with this cue, drop your hand dramatically the instant you feel his momentum slow—often before he comes to a complete stop. Drop your rein to his neck so he gets a clear and meaningful release from the cue. After teaching thousands of riders, I find that the most common error in using the one-rein stop is not releasing soon enough.

If your horse doesn't stop completely, pick up the same rein again and release again when you feel him slow. Do this until he's totally stopped.

Teaching the one-rein stop and giving the instant release will help your horse understand your stop cue and make it easy to stop without the bracing and pulling you get from two reins. If you need to use this cue in an emergency setting or when your horse becomes fractious, he'll know what to do and how to receive a release from the rein pressure.

It's critical to release your horse when he first makes an effort to slow down and stop; he'll often stop on the release rather than the pull. Timing is everything. The sooner you provide a release for your horse's willingness to slow and stop, the sooner he'll understand what to do and learn to follow directions.

At first, you may end up in a full turn as your horse disengages and stops. As you work on releasing the rein pressure at the right time, however, he'll soon learn to stop on the straightaway when you slightly lift one rein. As you practice, alternate right and left reins so he stops off either one.

Your horse usually wants to stop; he just doesn't always understand what to do and what

Step 2: Teach the Pulley-Rein Stop

your cues mean. By using only one rein and teaching him to stop with your release of pressure, he'll understand and obey quickly.

The one-rein stop is useful when your horse startles or jumps, but it isn't a good idea if your horse is bolting and running away with you at full speed. In that case, you'll want to use the pulley rein to stop your horse.

Step 2.
Teach the Pulley-Rein Stop
If you execute the pulley rein correctly, you can stop a runaway horse immediately. While this riding skill isn't for everyday use, the move can be lifesaving if your horse bolts, because you're intentionally applying leverage to his mouth.

Stopping with the pulley rein is far preferable to pulling an out-of-control horse into a circle with the one-rein stop. If your horse's flight instinct is fully engaged and he is running full-speed ahead, turning him sharply or cueing him for a one-rein stop may cause him to lose

his footing and fall down. This could be highly dangerous for the horse and rider.

The pulley-rein technique requires some practice, which can be risky and hard on your horse. In fact, many instructors don't like to teach this emergency-stop technique, especially with school horses that may have to endure practice over and over.

Keep your practice sessions short and consider practicing the rein movements without pulling dramatically. When you apply the rein-aid correctly, you'll be able to feel the stopping power you have without pulling your full strength.

When you execute this rein aid correctly, the stopping power is huge—make sure you release your horse the instant he stops. If he begins backing up and you fail to release the pressure, you could be in danger of pulling him over backward onto you. However, used correctly, it's a great tool to have in your bag of tricks. *(Continued on page 29.)*

Q&A
WITH JULIE

About Emergency Dismounting

Question: *If you want to stay on, at what moment does the rider decide to execute an emergency dismount?*

Answer: This is a good question and one to which there is no definitive answer—it all depends on the circumstance. In general, you are usually better off and safer to stay on the horse if it's at all possible. Even teaching the emergency dismount is somewhat controversial, for two reasons. First, practicing the emergency dismount is risky and injury prone; when vaulting off a moving horse, it's easy to fall down, sprain an ankle, or worse. So practicing something that you may not ever need, which may cause you injury just by the mere practicing of it, is a questionable endeavor. Of course, you could certainly argue the opposite: that if you were to ever need it, having practiced it may make you less prone to injury. When I taught kids, I had them learn and practice the emergency dismount routinely—it was fun! Now that my student base is middle-aged and older adults, I don't teach it at all—because of the potential for injury in the practice.

The second reason why it's controversial to teach the emergency dismount is because you may end up with a rider who bails off the horse for no good reason when he or she should have stayed on and this can cause a lot of problems, especially on the trail. Again, you are usually safer on the horse than off, because when you come off you are probably going to hit the ground (or some other hard object) and you may become a victim of the horse's

hooves. Out in the open, you may lose your horse and have a very long walk home. However, like everything with horses, there are exceptions to the rule.

The few times I have voluntarily done an emergency dismount, there have been some extenuating circumstances, and these are probably the only situations in which I would do it. In both instances I can remember, the horse was running away with me, out in the open—not in an arena—maybe bucking, maybe not, but I had already tried my best to regain control and determined I couldn't do it. Running away, in and of itself, is not enough to make me bail, because I learned riding race horses that eventually he will run out of oxygen and stop. In both cases when I did bail, the horse was headed for something dangerous, like a barb-wire fence, with seemingly no concern about his own well-being. Running away is one thing, but when the horse is in such a panic that he loses his sense of self-preservation, you're in trouble.

I think that if a rider is too quick to bail off, not only is she risking injury in the dismount but there will also be times when she could've stayed on if she had tried. But a controlled crash-landing is usually better than an uncontrolled one. I do think there is some value in learning how to take a fall—tuck and roll—don't brace for impact with your arms. And I think it's also valuable to

know the process of an emergency dismount.

There are two really critical factors when you are coming off a horse, whether it's an emergency dismount or not by choice. First, you have to get your feet clear of the stirrups ASAP. You'd be surprised how many people, in a panic, go to dismount and forget to take their feet out. The potential disastrous results are obvious. Secondly, DO NOT hold onto the reins—let the horse go! Many people try to hang onto the reins when they fall, in a last-ditch effort to maintain control, and then end up pulling the horse down onto them or breaking an arm or dislocating a shoulder. If you are coming off a horse, voluntarily or not, get your feet out of the stirrups and let go, pushing yourself as far away from the horse as possible.

It's an unfortunate characteristic of the sport that things sometimes do not go according to plan. And even with the most docile, steady horse, there may be times when bad things happen. Keeping your wits about you and continuing to think through the crisis are the most useful tools you have. The emergency dismount has its time and place, but it should be a method of last resort.

For more answers, visit the Training Library: www. juliegoodnight. com/ traininglibrary

To practice the pulley-rein stop, shorten one rein as tight as you can, and push that hand's knuckles into your horse's neck (as I demonstrate with my left hand in Photo 2A). Your hand should be braced and centered over the crest of the mane, with the rein very tight to prevent your horse's head from turning when you pull the other rein. This hand is the base of your "pulley," so keep it pressed into his neck; make sure you don't lift up as you pull back with the other rein.

Next, slide your other hand down the opposite rein, reaching as far forward as you can. It helps to hold the tail of this rein with the fingers that are braced into your horse's neck. Now, pull straight back and up toward your belly button with all your weight as you sit back deep into the saddle (Photo 2B).

Because the first rein is locked tight and braced, it prevents your horse's head from turning; he's suddenly pulling against his own neck. The pull on the second rein creates a lot of pressure on the side of his mouth, bending his neck slightly and causing him to stop. You're using your horse's weight against him, rather than pulling back on two reins using your own muscle power.

Practice going through the motions of the pulley rein—shorten and brace, shorten and pull—so that your movements become automatic. You won't need to use much pulling pressure as you practice; just practice your hand motions and gathering the reins correctly.

When the motions of the pulley rein become automatic, try practicing it out in the open field, where your horse may naturally get a little stronger in his gaits. Now you can play with the pressure a little bit to get a feel for the strength you have with this rein aid. Naturally, a bigger, stronger horse will need more pressure to stop.

With a little luck, you'll never need to use the pulley rein. But you never know what can happen out on the trail and it's definitely a good thing to know if you ever need it!

Walk This Way:
Stepping Out on the Trail

Teach your horse to walk at a steady pace that you determine.

Dually walks at the speed I dictate, whether we're moving away from or toward the barn.

IN OUR "HORSE MASTER" EPISODE entitled "Walk This Way," rider Sharon Cervantes wanted nothing more than to trail ride with her friends. The problem was, her adorable Quarter Horse gelding was slow. He was never in a hurry. That's a great quality in a horse at times. I'd usually prefer a horse with too much whoa instead of too much go; at the same time, you want to be able to ride *with* your friends and not always watch them seeing the scenery first. We all know that saying about what happens if you're not the lead dog. It's no fun being the one behind the group and having to yell for your friends to "wait up!" over and over, breaking into a trot regularly to keep up.

Amber Mathewson of Alabama, a previous cast member on "Horse Master," wrote in with a similar trail problem. "Because of personality differences, I seem to always [prefer] slow walking and lazy horses, and my husband always [prefers] speed walking and got-to-be-in-the-front horses. That has created a lot of trouble for me when my horse gets far behind my speed-walking husband. If the other horse is too far ahead, my horse gets anxious, antsy, and thinks he can trot ahead to catch up—without my speed-up cue."

Your horse should move at the pace and gait you choose. You shouldn't have to alternate constantly between a walk and trot. Use these tips and strategies to make sure you know how to give your horse a "speed up the walk" cue so you can stay with your group and enjoy your ride.

As a trail rider, you ride your horse most often at a walk. But do you set the pace for the walk? Or does your horse decide how fast he should go—walking sluggishly away from the barn, keeping you at the back of the pack, and picking up the pace as soon as you turn for home? Does he lag behind the other horses then bust into a ground-pounding trot to catch up?

Do you feel sometimes that you have to constantly "pedal" your horse, and that you are doing more work than he is? Chances are he's learned that he gets to make decisions, he's in charge, and you're merely sitting on top for a ride.

To help you be a fully engaged rider, I will teach you more about the walking gait, how to feel it, and how to cue your horse for the extended walk using natural aids so he's always moving at the speed *you* determine.

If your horse speeds up on the way back to the barn, you know that he can walk quickly. It's up to you to teach him that he can walk just as fast when you're heading out and while ambling down the trail.

The walk is a four-beat lateral gait without *suspension*. That is, your horse always has at least two hooves on the ground and usually three, so there's no moment when all hooves are off the ground (as there is during the trot and lope/canter); therefore, you never feel a bounce. For example, he'll place his right hind foot, then the right fore, then left hind, then left fore foot on the ground, creating a lateral, or side-to-side, rhythm. Each foot placement creates an equal beat: 1-2-3-4.

The walk is a gait to be mastered and refined, not just a warm-up for faster speeds. It's the best gait for riding over any precarious or hilly terrain, because your horse needs his feet

Walk This Way

Horsemanship lesson: Teach your horse to walk at the pace of your choosing.

Why you need it on the trail: When you start out from the barn, or when you're at the back of your trail group, your horse may think that he calls the shots and can walk slowly, determining the speed and how much energy he uses. He needs to follow your lead when it comes to direction and speed.

What you'll do: You'll learn to feel your horse's hoofbeats at the walk and become aware of how your body moves in response to each beat. You'll use your body's natural rhythm to help your horse speed up to the pace that you choose and maintain the gait. If he has an ingrained habit of ignoring your directions, you may need to reinforce your natural leg aids with a crop or the tail of reins.

What you'll need: Your saddle and bridle, and either split reins with a long *bight* (tail), romal reins, which have a quirt at the end, or a short crop.

Step 1: Feel Your Horse's Speed

on the ground for balance as he navigates over logs or around branches and holes.

As you learn to feel the walk's beats and rate your horse's speed, you'll gain confidence as a rider and teach your horse that you're the one in charge.

Step 1.
Feel Your Horse's Speed

Outfit your horse in the tack listed in the box on page 31. Mount up, and ask your horse to walk away from the barn. Study his walking gait and make sure he's listening to your speed cues.

Make sure you are sitting in correct position, sitting well back, with your pelvis open and your lower back flat and relaxed. Notice how much your hips move from side to side as your horse walks (at a slow walk, you may not feel much motion). If you're riding with a buddy, notice how far your horse is from the lead. If he's holding back and allowing the other horse to get ahead easily, he may be cheating you.

Then ask your horse to speed up by reaching forward, closing contact with your legs and increasing the driving rhythm in your seat. Does

he react with a faster walk? Or does he become confused and begin to trot? If he doesn't speed up his walk while maintaining the gait, perfect your speed cues with the exercises that follow.

If you have trouble deciding if your horse is walking too slowly, ask a friend to watch your horse's feet. If your horse has little forward motion, drags his toes, doesn't "track up" by placing his hind feet near where his front feet just landed, or hesitates between steps, it's time to work on the walk (in Photo 1A, note the position of the horse's hesitatingly slow feet).

When your horse begins to walk faster, he'll pick his feet up higher and step farther. The rhythm of his walk will increase and he'll have more impulsion (in Photo 1B, note the horse's right front foot has moved ahead and his back feet are poised for action).

Step 2.
Apply Natural Aids

Make sure you're sitting in a proper horsemanship position with your car, shoulder, hip, and heel in alignment and your lower back flat, relaxed, and in a vertical position. In this position, feel how your back and hips move laterally (side-to-side) and vertically (up-and-down) with your horse as he walks.

Begin to exaggerate your movements so that your hips and legs are swinging with your horse's barrel. Feel your hips as they move forward and down one at a time. When your right hip lifts, your horse is pushing off with his right hind leg. As your right hip rises, your left hip drops so that your left leg closes contact on your horse's barrel.

I like to exaggerate this movement to show how the movement of your horse affects your position. Notice how my right hip rises and my right leg moves away from my horse as my left hip and leg drop down close to my horse's side (Photo 2A). On the next step (Photo 2B), my left hip rises and my right leg falls closer to my horse.

Important: If you're not feeling the movement in your horse's back, you may be riding with your pelvis tipped forward. When your pelvis is in this closed position, you can't feel your horse's back movements. To fix this position flaw, simply sit back on your seat bones

(visualize sitting on the back-pocket stitching of your jeans), suck your belly button in toward your spine and relax your lower back.

Now that you understand this natural cause and effect, you also know the proper timing to apply natural aids and prompt your horse to lengthen the walk. When each leg closes against your horse's side, it's time to apply alternating lower leg pressure, cueing him to move forward with more energy and impulsion. Because your hips are moving in a side-to-side fashion, your horse understands that he's to remain at a walk. If he steps into a trot when you give the speed-up cue, immediately bring him back to a walk and ask again for him to lengthen the walk.

Continue to alternate your leg aids in a natural rhythm and gradually apply more leg pressure as you increase the rhythm in your hips. When your horse responds by lengthening the walk, soften your leg pressure, but continue the rhythm with your seat. Your horse should maintain the rhythm you set with your seat.

Note: Depending on your horse, you may need to add a little bump with your calf to get

Step 2: Apply Natural Aids

2A

2B

Step 3: Keep the Pace

the response you're looking for. Don't worry if he mistakes your cue and starts to trot; simply correct him with your seat and hands. Bring him back to a walk, and ask again for a more ener-getic walk. In time, and with consistent corrections, he'll understand what you mean.

Step 3.
Keep the Pace

When you ask your horse to speed up, he should maintain that speed until you give him a new cue. Notice in Photo 3A that my right hip is raised (note the fold in my vest on my right), but I'm not exaggerating my leg position as shown previously. My horse is moving forward nicely as shown by his leg placement. Two of his hooves are on the ground, one is ready to step down and one is pushing off, showing that he's in constant motion and not walking slowly, as in Photo 1A.

If you find yourself applying leg pressure with every step to keep your horse moving ahead, you're "pedaling" your horse. A properly trained horse is trained to continue performing a task until told to do something new. If you're not getting any speed response from your horse

after applying your leg aids, he's learned that he doesn't have to respond. There's no consequence to staying at the speed he chooses and he's being willfully disobedient. If he's been trained not to obey in this way, he might need a gentle spank with the reins or a crop. A gentle spank with the crop (or with the tail of the reins as seen in photo 3B) reinforces the leg aid, so it should be used right where you gave him the leg cue on his ribs.

Either of these artificial aids, the crop or the ends of the reins, will simply reinforce your leg aid and train your horse to listen to a cue as soon as it's given. Use only the amount of pressure necessary to motivate your horse to try harder. A soft bump may be all the pressure required.

To reinforce your leg aid with split reins, hold them in one hand, and pick up the tail with your other hand. After asking your horse to move forward with your leg cue and getting no response, gently flop the rein tail beside your right leg or toward his hindquarters. Just make sure you have enough rein to do this without inadvertently pulling back on the reins—which is a slow-down cue. *(Continued on page 36.)*

Old and Tired

Question: *I got my Quarter Horse a year and a half ago from the barn where I used to ride, and he's about 15 years old. They sold the farm and wanted to give their horses to good homes, and Zip was one of the horses I used to ride. He basically was a walk-trot horse for the younger kids so he's very dead to any of the aids I give him. I've tried some of your techniques–urging him on with my seat, then kicking, and as a last resort I pop him just to make him walker faster, but it always seems to be a struggle. I'm not afraid of hard work and I have determination, but he sometimes gets the best of me. I've also tried asking him to canter and he's not too happy with me; he's now bucked me off three times. I think he's very happy with his walk-trot life, but I would like a little more. He picks up the correct lead, but it's a workout for me just to keep him going, and when I feel him slow down and try to urge him on or go to the crop, that's when the mean Zip comes out. I thought maybe he was ring sour, so I took him out into a field and we cantered once, twice, but the third was the kicker and no pun intended. He gets this little bug up his butt and, phew! I go flying off. Of course, now I'm a little intimidated when I ask him to canter. I'm trying to be "the captain" but I think it'll take more time!*

Answer: Speeding up a slow horse is an easier problem to fix than slowing down a fast horse, but nonetheless, it can be a challenge, as you have seen with your old beginner's horse. You raise some interesting issues, which I see as: 1) you may want more from your horse than he is capable of or willing to give you; 2) you may have gotten greedy in his training; and 3) you now have a leadership and confidence issue with your horse.

If your horse was represented to you as a 15-year-old, I'd be willing to bet a huge wad of cash that he is considerably older. Horses are almost always older than we think they are, and without registration papers it can be difficult to pin down the horse's exact age. Your horse has been a champion beginner's walk-trot horse for many years and it may not be reasonable to try to make him into something he's not, just because that is what you want, especially when he is good at his job.

You cannot fit a square peg into a round hole. What makes him a good beginner's horse is exactly what you are fighting: laziness. It's not that an older horse cannot be retrained—he can; but as you have seen, it requires a skilled rider with good timing, authority, and confidence, because he is very set in his ways (both physically and mentally). So, my first suggestion to you is that you consider moving on to a horse who is more suitable to your riding goals at this time. It's always easy to find a good home for a decent beginner's horse.

The fact that your horse has bucked you off three times does not bode well for your ability to correct this behavior. Every time a horse has success (gets released from pressure), he learns something. You cannot unlearn what the horse already knows. I wish I could take back all the times I have gotten greedy in my training and asked for something once, twice, three times, and then regretted it.

It's a hard training concept to grasp, but rewarding the horse with good timing is critical; that means not asking over and over, but being happy when you get the response you asked for and moving onto something else. Asking repeatedly usually unravels the horse's responsiveness. Rather than asking your horse to canter three times in a row, I'd ask him for short spells of canter throughout his workout, always looking for the opportunity to reward him (let him stop) when he is compliant (moving the way I want).

If he moves into the canter when I cue and goes a few strides forward, I might stop him and let him rest and do something easy. A little while later, I'll ask again, making sure I only stop him when he is moving the way I want. Gradually, over time, I would ask for a stride more until he is cantering all the way around without resistance. By giving him time, he has gotten in the habit of being obedient without a big fight and he has gotten some conditioning to make it physically easier for him too. Every time the horse has been released for doing the wrong thing (like bucking or resisting), he has scored major

To reinforce your leg aid with a crop, simply carry the crop in your non-reining hand, and have it ready to tap on your horse's barrel, right where your leg cued him. Start with the least amount of pressure, then escalate the pressure until you find the amount it takes to get a response. Don't continually use the reins or crop in the same way if the pressure isn't causing an effect. Increase pressure until you see a result.

Important: I often see riders pull back on the reins as they apply an artificial aid. You've asked your horse to speed up, so make sure that you don't pull on his mouth, giving mixed cues. You should always reach forward with your rein hand, toward the horse's ears, whenever you want him to move more forward.

When you're riding in rhythm with your horse and he's responsive to your speed-up cues, you'll have a trail partner who can cover ground while you ride in comfort. Keep your hips swaying from side to side to feel your horse's rhythm, then apply leg pressure only when needed; your horse should come to the rhythm of your seat.

Old and Tired (continued)

points (sometimes big ones from the sounds of it), so you are starting the training game already seriously behind on the score. There are several Q&As on my website about horses that buck at canter and about a training concept called "ask, tell, command," which will help you with your training goals.

Your horse is unresponsive to the leg and has learned that he can sull-up and outlast anything that you can dish out in an effort to get him moving. As soon as you take a break in the kicking or hitting (from exhaustion), he is rewarded. This is extremely common in beginner horses and is not hard for an expert to fix. There are also lots of Q&As on my website that talk about motivating a horse to change his behavior. The more set a horse is in his ways, the more motivation (pressure) it's likely to take to change his behavior and the more likely he is to resist the change.

It requires a strong and confident rider to dish out the appropriate pressure that motivates the horse and to ride through the aftermath when the horse's temper flares. There is an old saying in horse training, "It always gets worse before it gets better." That means a horse with established behavior is not likely to give it up just because you put your foot down; he will resist until he is convinced that his efforts are futile. Your horse has already had a great deal of success in not having to canter, so he has reason to be convinced otherwise.

You don't have to give up on this horse, but I think you need to be more realistic in what you ask of him. You need to back way up and just ask for good transitions from halt to walk, so that he transitions with very little seat and leg pressure. Before you begin working on cantering, your halt-walk-slow trot-fast trot transitions should be smooth and the horse should be moving obediently off your leg. Timing of the release and the appropriate amount of pressure are critical to success and, unfortunately, that is not something I can help you adjust without seeing you and your horse in action.

Any horse whose behavior you are trying to change must be able to "see the light" and figure out what he has to do to get out of the pressure and to make his life peaceful and comfortable. That is why in natural horsemanship we have the concept of "make the right thing easy and the wrong thing hard." Sometimes it's important to focus on rewarding him when he is good, rather than punishing the bad, so he knows and looks for the easy part of the equation.

For more answers, visit the Training Library: www.juliegoodnight.com/traininglibrary

Ride to the Side:
Improve Your Sidepassing Skills

How to "open and shut doors" to put your horse where you want him to go.

On the trail, sidepassing is an important skill. Here, Dually and I practice our sidepass training.

ONE NIGHT WHEN I WAS OUT to dinner with some horsewomen, we happened upon the topic of pet peeves. What are your pet peeves, and what do you hate to see when it comes to trail riding? The conversation included everything from silly bugaboos to serious safety issues. The topic that struck me, though, was the mention of riders who only know how to ride straight ahead—and don't have control of their horse's every step so that they have the ability to navigate tricky terrain.

Don't get me wrong: I think that many trail riders are excellent riders who want to do the best for their horses. There is a stigma and stereotype out there, though, that trail riders sit back, relax, go for a ride, and have little control of their horses. Let's do our best to prove that stereotype wrong—completely wrong. There are skills from the arena that are good to know on the trail. Sidepassing is one of those important skills. If you haven't taken time to practice skills that are commonly thought of as "show" maneuvers, it's time to get to work at home so that you can get out of any messes you may find yourself in on the trail.

Why would you need to sidepass on the trail? One day, you might ride too close to a broken bottle and need to step away from the glass. You might want to ride up closer to a mailbox to get the mail—or close to a fence to set your jacket down. Or you may need to navigate around a rock when a ledge blocks your backward movement. Sidepassing is important for establishing total body control over your horse (not just control of his nose) and it could be very useful for riding out on the ranch or if you ever needed to sort cattle. The more you know how to cue your horse—and develop the skills to control your horse's every step and every move—the closer you get to being a great horseperson.

W hen you teach your horse to sidepass, you learn to control his every foot placement, guide his every step, and have total body control. If you teach your horse this skill correctly, he'll respond to your every cue and to your *natural aids* (seat, hand, and leg) and you'll develop the ability to position your horse exactly where you want him.

In this lesson, I'll teach you how to position your body and use your aids so that your horse will quickly understand that you're asking for sideways movement. I'll show you how to practice this new skill using a fence line as a guide.

Step 1.
Learn the Cues

Tack up (see bit recommendation, box at left), and warm up as usual. Practice transitions (changes of speed or gait) and turning to make sure your horse is listening to your cues.

In this step, you'll learn how to use your body to ask your horse for this precise maneuver. In the next step, you'll introduce him to the training process by using the cue.

Keep in mind that there are only six ways a horse can move: forward, back, through the right shoulder, through the right hip, through the left shoulder, and through the left hip. Imagine these

Ride to the Side

Horsemanship lesson: You'll learn how to use your primary natural aids—your seat, legs, and hands—to cue the horse to move sideways. You'll apply these aids to control his every step.

Why you need it on the trail: On the trail, sidepassing is an important skill. Without it, you may find yourself in a jam when you need to dodge through timber and tight openings or sidle next to another rider to offer aid. Sidepassing also comes in handy when it's time to open a gate, drag a log, pony another horse, push aside brush, and avoid a rock or even a snake.

What you'll do: You'll begin by learning how to position your body so that your horse will understand the go-sideways cue. Next, you'll reinforce your sidepass cues as you ride next to a fence or barrier to help him understand which direction to go. When you've mastered your work on the fence line, you'll progress to sidepassing over a ground pole and logs.

What you'll need: If your horse hasn't been trained to sidepass at all, it's best to start out with a snaffle bit or a curb bit with articulation between the shanks (rather than a solid mouthpiece). A bit with movement that works off the sides of the horse's mouth will help him feel your side-to-side rein aids better.

Skills your horse will need: Your horse needs to know how to stop with just a seat cue, go forward off your leg cue, and back up on cue, going straight and moving with energy.

directions as the "doors" that you can open and close with your leg and rein aids. To start, we'll open the doors to the right and close the doors to the front, back, and left.

Pick up the reins and shift your weight back slightly to block your horse's forward motion (that is, close the door to the front). For a sidepass to the right (shown at right), open the right rein to the side (lift it slightly to encourage your horse to lift his shoulder), and move your left hand to his neck's midline (closing the "door" to movement to the left and opening a passageway to the right). *Note:* never cross your hand over the midline of the horse's neck—it will interfere with his movement and pull his nose the wrong way.

Open your right leg by stretching your foot to the right (be careful not to stiffen or brace this leg). Close your left leg on his rib cage, and bump your calf muscle against his side.

By disallowing forward movement with your hands, opening your right aids, and closing your left aids, your horse will move toward the opening, that is, to the right.

Make sure you release the cue on the slightest effort of the horse—even if he just bows his rib cage in the right direction. The release will tell him that is the right direction to move and, with subsequent cues, he will understand more easily. Ask, then release—ask, then release.

Step 1: Learn the Cues

Step 2.
Use a Fence Line

Now that you know how to position your body, it's time to teach your horse to move sideways. For this, you'll need the help of a fence. Use a safe, solid fence to face him into to remind him to move sideways and that there's no option to move forward.

Fence work will give you a visual guide to work with and provide a natural barrier to block your horse's forward movement. The fence will help you stay straight, or perpendicular to the fence, and you'll also make sure that you're truly moving to the left or right and quickly make any corrections to your horse's body position.

Walk your horse up to a fence, and stop him with his nose to the rail and his body perpendicular to the fence. Keeping his body straight and perpendicular to the fence, ask him to sidepass using your opening and closing aids.

As soon as any movement occurs, release the cue, and return to a neutral sitting position. Reward

Passing a Groundwork Test

Question: *Help! My daughter, who's 14, enrolled her 2-year-old Arabian gelding in a 4-H ground-training project and intends to show him this summer at our county fair. In one of the required tests, she has to sidepass him over a ground pole, without touching his body for cueing. How does a person teach this skill?*

Answer: Horses are very good at learning and responding to hand signals; that's what you'll use to sidepass your horse from the ground without touching him. In the herd, horses communicate primarily with gestures and postures. They're used to looking for clues about what you're communicating because they would look for cues from others in the herd. When I begin groundwork training with any horse, I use very specific hand signals—even if the horse doesn't yet know what they mean. I point to the right when I want the horse to go right or point to the left when I want the horse to go left—just as you might gesture to someone you are walking with to show them where to go. I have one hand signal for backing, one for coming to me, and I use my hands very specifically when I want the horse to speed up or slow down. With a little time, the horse picks up the subtle cues and I can move any part of the horse's body by just pointing to it. This idea is what you'll use for your sidepassing cue.

Horses learn hand signals (like pointing to his shoulder) when you reinforce your signal with other aids (swinging the rope or tapping him with a stick). By using the hand signal first (this works the same to teach a voice cue), then reinforcing the cue, the horse quickly learns that if he responds to the hand signal, the reinforcement won't be necessary.

You shouldn't use the hand signal (or a voice cue) repeatedly—give the horse one chance to respond, then reinforce with stronger aids.

As you do groundwork with horses, the primary focus is on moving the horse out of your space. As your horse learns to yield to your space, he becomes more respectful of your authority and starts looking to you for advice on where he should go and what he should do. This is a natural behavior of horses and you see it all the time in the herd as the dominant horses gesture to other horses to move away. As I do groundwork with horses, I like to focus on controlling four parts of the horse's body—his nose, his shoulder, his hip, and his feet. When you can control all four parts of the horse, you'll be able to ask him to go forward, backward, or sideways by just gesturing. But he has to know that you will reinforce the hand signals with stronger aids, before he bothers to look for or respond to your hand signals.

You'll lay the foundation for sidepassing by doing much simpler exercises with your horse, like leading, circling, backing, and moving the shoulder or hip away from you. As you work on fundamental leading skills, the horse will learn to focus on what your hands and posture are doing for information on what he's supposed to do (speed up, slow down, stop, turn).

Your horse will learn that he has to maintain a specific position in relationship to you, like a dog that learns to heel. As you lead, you should always turn the horse away from you, to reinforce him moving out of your space, and the more responsive your horse becomes, the tighter and quicker the turns should be, until the horse begins to cross over his front legs and pivot on the hindquarters. Thus, you are gaining control of his shoulders.

It will be helpful to use a flag or stick (a 48-inch rigid rod) in the beginning so that when you gesture with your hand for the horse to move away, he sees the stick waving at him. You may even need to reinforce the gesture by touching him or tapping him with the stick. If I want the horse to move his shoulder, I focus on his shoulder and point the stick right at it as I move toward his shoulder and cluck. If he doesn't move that part of his body away, the stick will run into him. After a few reinforcements with the stick, your horse will learn to respond to the hand signal by moving his shoulder away before anything touches him.

Early on in your groundwork, you should learn how to disengage the horse's hindquarters and make him take a step away from you with his hind end, crossing over his hind

(continued on page 42)

your horse with a release and a pat no matter how small the sidestep he takes. This lets him know that he moved in the correct direction and will help him understand the cue.

Pause briefly, then ask your horse to move to the right once again. As soon as he steps to the side, however small the step, reward him with a quick release of cues and a pat. When he associates your new cue with moving sideways, you can begin to ask for more steps before rewarding him.

After you've finished working to the right, repeat these steps to ask for a sidepass to the left. That is, open the doors to the left, while closing the doors to the right, front, and back. Do not switch back and forth from right to left while he's still learning; it's easier for a horse to learn on one side at a time.

When your horse understands your sidepass cue and is responding well (that is, he'll easily take two or three steps sideways before needing encouragement), ask him to sidepass a longer distance.

Troubleshooting tips: As you begin to teach your horse to sidepass, he may (1) move forward or back too much; (2) move his shoulder in front of his hips (this is most common and causes a turn instead of a sidepass), or (3) move his hip before his shoulder.

To fix these problems, use your aids either to block movement of your horse's body part or to encourage more movement of another body part. For instance, if your horse moves his shoulders too far and lags with his hip, block his shoulder a little by closing with your right rein and using your left rein to encourage hip movement.

To do so, bring your right hand back toward his neck to block the shoulder (don't pull back), and bring your left hand back and up toward your belly button in an "indirect rein" to move the hip. At the same time, reach back more with your outside leg, and bump his side to encourage his hip to move. If needed, apply slight backward equal rein pressure to close the door to forward movement.

Step 2: Use a Fence Line

Anytime your horse moves correctly, or tries extra hard, reward him with a release and a pat. Moving laterally isn't easy for him and learning this skill can be stressful, so don't overdo it. Once you get a few steps, reward him and end on a good note.

If your horse gets nervous or irritable when working on this, he's feeling too much pressure–physical and mental. Slow down, shorten your training sessions, and reward him for a smaller number of steps.

Work on a sidepass to the right until your horse is compliant (Photos 2A and 2B). Repeat to the left. Because of the one-sided nature of

Passing a Groundwork Test *(continued)*

legs. Again, by pointing toward his hip, moving toward him, and shaking the flag at him, he'll learn the cue. It's really important for the horse to learn to yield his hip, since it is the opposite of kicking. While you are teaching this to your horse, be careful. It would not be unusual for the horse to become defensive and want to kick out. As long as you are not within kicking range, it won't matter if he does kick out.

Throughout all of this training, you should think of your gestures as cues that you are willing to reinforce and not as movements to force your horse to do something. You'll practice until you can move the horse's nose, shoulder, and hip away from you by just pointing at that part of his body.

When you can do this, you have all the skills you need for sidepassing. All you have to do is point at his hip with one hand and point at his shoulder with the other hand and he'll know to yield both his shoulder and hip at the same time. When you are ready to sidepass, it will be helpful to lead your horse up to a fence, nose to the rail, just like you would if you were teaching sidepassing from the saddle. This will eliminate forward as an option and help the horse understand the cue sooner.

To practice, stand at his side—in the middle of his body—with a slack lead in the hand nearest his head. Then start gesturing with both hands—one finger pointing directly at his shoulder and one hand pointing directly at his hip. Take a step toward him and cluck at him to let him know you expect him to move. Watch his barrel closely and at the first indication that he's yielding his body, release the cue and praise him. You won't necessarily wait until he steps sideways; at the first sign he's thinking about moving in the right direction, release the cue and praise your horse.

He'll learn the cue much more quickly that way. Ask again and release and reward any movement in the correct direction. Soon, he'll be stepping sideways with both the shoulder and hip but you'll want to keep releasing after just one step until you are getting that reliably and effortlessly; then you can start asking for two steps at a time. Take your time and be slow and systematic with your horse—you don't want him to develop anxiety and resistance and you want to be able to control each and every step. Through frequent releases and lots of praise, he'll learn to love it and eagerly look for the cue.

As with any skill you teach your horse, you'll have to teach it on both sides. Start with the left side—side-passing to the right—since he's most used to you handling him from that side. Practice for 5 to 10 minutes on that side, then give your horse a break by doing something easier, then come back and practice on the off side. Switching from side to side is more challenging for the horse. Since he's learning a new skill, it's best to work on one side at a time. Because learning to sidepass can be stressful for some horses, be careful not to overdo the practice and stay vigilant for signs of stress—reverting to something easier if your horse becomes anxious.

Since neither the horse nor your daughter knows how to do this, you may need the help of a more experienced handler to school the horse and supervise your daughter to avoid problems and miscues, and to make sure your daughter stays in a safe position and does not get kicked. My video "Lead Line Leadership" demonstrates and explains all the skills needed to achieve this goal.

For more answers, visit the Training Library: www. juliegoodnight. com/ traininglibrary

the horse's brain, when you are teaching a new skill, it's best to work on one side until you are finished, then proceed to train the other side. Switching back and forth is difficult when the horse is first learning, but once he is finished in the skill, you can switch back and forth. Gradually increase the number of steps until he can sidepass 10 to 15 steps while staying fairly straight through his body.

When your horse is moving well off your aids, try sidepassing away from the fence, with his tail near the fence and his nose pointed away (Photo 2C). Focus on keeping him straight through his body so that his shoulders and hips are fairly even. In this position, he won't have the fence to guide him visually, but you can easily note and correct any straightness problems. Note: If your horse has a tendency to back up instead of move sideways, turn his tail to the fence sooner. After you are getting a good sidepass near the fence, it's time to try it out in the open.

Step 3.
Add a Ground Pole

As your horse progresses, test your sidepassing skills over a ground pole. Work to keep the pole between your horse's front and back feet, or even with your shoulder. You'll quickly notice any idiosyncrasies if your horse steps forward or back. Go slowly at first, moving one step at a time so your horse does not learn to rush through and move haphazardly.

Work one direction and then the other, and always remember to stop and praise your horse for his efforts. Ride around the pole, then return to sidepass over it, in front of it, or behind it. Then he won't learn that his feet must always be over a pole.

When your horse easily sidepasses over a ground pole, progress to sidepassing over

Step 3: Add a Ground Pole

larger logs on the trail. Look for other opportunities to sidepass, such as moving toward a post to pick up a slicker or rope or negotiate around a bush.

Having complete body control of your horse is of the utmost importance in trail riding, especially if you find yourself in more challenging terrain or being in charge of other horses and riders. You'll find this skill comes in handy in a variety of instances, and you'll love the maneuverability of your well-trained trail horse.

Ride on Through:
Open and Close a Gate from Horseback

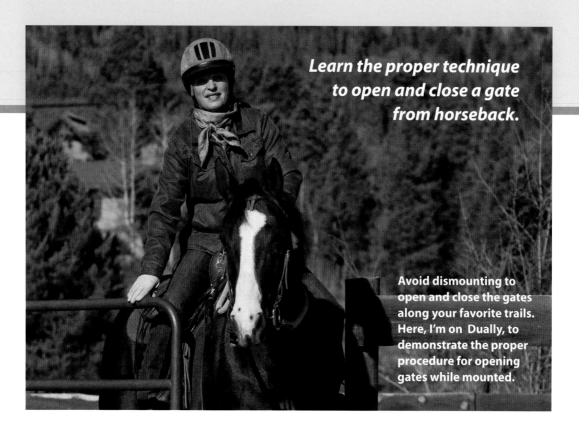

Learn the proper technique to open and close a gate from horseback.

Avoid dismounting to open and close the gates along your favorite trails. Here, I'm on Dually, to demonstrate the proper procedure for opening gates while mounted.

STANDING TALL AT 5 FEET 4 INCHES, I do my best to stay in shape and pride myself on being able to step into the stirrup—from the ground—no matter how tall the horse. My record-setting mount was getting on a giant horse during a presentation at Equine Affaire; the horse was over 18 hands. Mounting blocks can be great if you're riding in the arena, but you can't take them with you once you're on the trail. While I can jump on and off pretty easily, I still don't want to get down from my horse unless I absolutely have to. I expect all of my horses to be patient and listen to my cues as we open the gate to and from the arena and to and from the fields that lead us to our trails.

Heather Browne is an avid trail rider and often helps behind the scenes on "Horse Master." You'll also see her horse, Slide, in many of my photographs. Heather is about my height and rides a fairly tall Quarter Horse. She agrees that getting on and off to work a gate on the trail is annoying and promises to work on her gate-opening skills. "It's very frustrating to have to get down to open or close gates . . . especially since I usually need a mounting block just to get in the saddle with Slide! When I'm riding with a group of friends, we usually nominate the person with the smallest horse to be the one to get down and open the gate. I know that I need to work on mounting, and I need to work on opening gates."

I know you can learn the gate-opening skill and give up your frustrations on the trail. I'll help you break this often-overwhelming task into very doable parts.

As an avid trail rider, you probably have run across closed gates. When you learn to open and close a gate from horseback, you'll save time and energy and it will be easier for both you and your horse without more dismounting and remounting. You'll also teach your horse to willingly obey your precise cues as you gain greater control of his whole body.

Ride on Through

Horsemanship lesson: You'll learn the proper sequence to open, ride through, and close a gate, while keeping your horse methodical, responsive, and in control.

Why you need it on the trail: Knowing how to work a gate from the saddle will save you time and energy. It'll also save your horse from enduring frequent dismounts and mounts, which can be hard on his back.

What you'll do: You'll begin by gathering your reins and riding one-handed, then keeping hold of the gate in your free hand as you open it, ride through, make a U-turn around the gate to close the panel, and secure the latch.

What you'll need: Look for a metal panel gate that's easy to access, so you can ride up close alongside it without needing to practice your sidepassing skills. Find a gate you can open with your dominant hand (after you've mastered the first direction, you'll turn and work the gate in the reverse approach).

I recommend learning on a panel gate that opens in both directions so that your horse sees the obstacle and learns the correct movements. It's easy for your horse to step in the wrong place as a rope gate sways and bends. If you don't have a panel gate, you can craft a gate with two standards and a rope looped on a hook (when you can handle a solid gate, rope gates will be easy).

Also, look for a gate that opens with a push instead of a pull—or one that can swing in both directions, so you can eventually practice with the gate on your right or left side. It's not a good idea to pull a gate toward you—you should always use a push-to-open approach. Pulling the gate toward you can scare your horse and cause him to hit his legs on the gate.

Note: Don't practice on any gate made from wire (barbed or straight); your horse may injure himself (or you) on the metal spikes. Also, clear any nearby obstacles so that your horse doesn't bump into sharp objects or learn to fear riding so close to large equipment.

Skills your horse will need: Your horse should know how to move forward and back with light, precise cues. You'll also need to know how to turn sharply and step his hip to the side (turn on the forehand).

Your horse doesn't necessarily need to sidepass to get through a gate (but you may want to review Lesson 6 on sidepassing for better body control). You'll only need to do so if there isn't room to walk close to the fence line, then straight ahead to the gate's latch. However, sidepassing skills come in handy if you need to maneuver around trees or bushes to reach the gate and you should have enough body control of your horse that you can sidepass.

Step 1: Prep & Placement

In this lesson, I'll demonstrate the proper gate-opening procedure. Gate openings should be smooth and methodical, not rushed and disorganized.

Your horse needs to follow your commands and move deliberately, in case you're handling a tricky gate. If done incorrectly, your horse may bang his legs (or your knees) on the gate—or you may be tempted to lean dangerously out of the saddle, which puts severe torque on your horse's back. If your horse hits his legs, he may become anxious about future gate openings, and even learn to balk at gates, or rush through them.

Step 1.
Prep & Placement

Outfit your horse in his usual riding gear, and ride along your fence toward the panel gate. To open a gate with your right hand (shown), shorten the reins, and gather them in your left hand (Photo 1A). Leave just enough rein length so you can signal your horse easily without

putting undue pressure on his mouth or lifting your hand too high.

Note: You may opt to practice your one-handed reining and adjusting rein length in an open area *before* approaching the gate.

Ride toward the fence, and turn your horse so that his body is parallel to the gate. With the gate on your right, ride toward the latch, and stop when your shoulder is even with the latch—your horse's nose will be beyond the gate opening (Photo 1B). In this position, you won't have to reach for the latch and throw your body out of a balanced position, which can torque your horse's back.

Undo the latch, then put your hand on the gate's top rail. Your hand shouldn't leave the top rail of the gate until you've closed and latched it.

Next, back your horse toward the gate's hinges as you slide your hand back along the gate's top rail. Back up far enough so that your horse's nose will clear the gate post when you move forward and ride through the gate. From this position, you'll be ready to push the gate open.

Step 2.
Slow & Steady

Begin to push the gate open as you walk forward and turn your horse to the right toward the opening (Photo 2A). After your horse turns a step, stop and relax for a count of 10. This will help teach your horse that the gate-opening process is slow and deliberate.

Make sure your horse only steps forward on your command. If he takes an unauthorized step, he doesn't see you as the leader and will eventually speed through the gate—which could be dangerous if you catch your leg in the rungs.

When you're ready, calmly cue your horse to walk forward as you push the gate farther and walk toward the end of the panel. Continue to slide your hand along the gate's top rail, so the gate doesn't bump into your leg or your horse's side. Be prepared to stop when you reach the gate's end.

Don't ever allow your horse to nudge the gate open with his nose—this is unacceptable behavior and shows that he's impatient.

Step 2: Slow & Steady

Step 3.
Pivot & Hold

Again, make sure your horse listens to your cues and doesn't speed around the gate. Ask him to move forward then turn sharply to the right in a U-turn, pivoting around the gate's end and your right arm (Photos 3A and 3B).

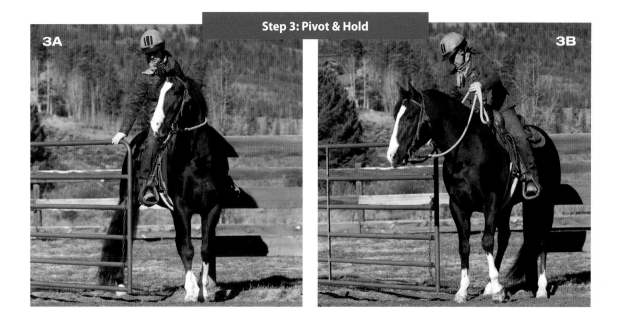

Step 3: Pivot & Hold

After you've completed your U-turn around the end of the gate—allowing your horse's front legs and hind legs to move as needed—walk forward a step or two toward the gate's hinges. Hold onto the gate's top rail and begin to push it closed as you walk forward toward the fence at about a 45-degree angle.

Step 4.
Close the Gate

Move your horse's hindquarters toward the gate (Photo 4A), completing a step or two of a turn on the forehand. Your horse's front legs will remain in the same spot as his hips move toward the gate. Back up, if necessary, after your turn on the

Practice portions of the gate-opening method, so your horse doesn't anticipate (and speed through) the process.

Expert Tips

- Practice opening and closing the gate each time you enter an arena and each time you head out to ride.

- Practice portions of gate-opening, so your horse doesn't anticipate (and speed through) the process. For instance, begin to open the gate, then ride away. Or, open the gate, ride through, then stop and hang out a moment, rather than immediately closing and latching the gate.

- Avoid developing a routine of opening and closing the gate before riding straight to the barn. Work your horse a little in the open, and close the gate several times in a row, so your horse doesn't become agitated and fast, thinking that gate work means it's time to go home.

- Practice controlling each step your horse takes, both when you're near the gate and away from it. Ask him to move forward, backward, and turn on his haunches and his forehand. Never let your horse walk or take a step without a cue.

forehand, so that he's parallel to the fence line and your shoulder is even with the gate's latch (Photo 4B).

Ask your horse to stand still as you stand near the latch. Count to 10 or higher so your horse learns to stand still as you take your time to latch the gate (Photo 4C). This will help avoid the common problem of the horse rushing off as you are trying to latch the gate.

When you and your horse get the hang of a normal gate opening—and you've taught him to wait for your cues—then you can start working a gate with your non-dominant hand, and move on to working a rope-and-post gate. Master your precision and straightness on a rigid gate before you approach a "flexible" gate, so your horse does not develop the squirrelly habits that he might get away with on a rope gate.

Step 4: Close the Gate

Q&A WITH JULIE

Help with Leg Cues

Question: *How should I use my legs to cue my horse? I learned to ride with just my reins to cue and I know I need to know more skills to cue my horse with my whole body.*

Answer: For riders learning to use the aids to stop and go, I teach the "gears of the seat": neutral, forward, and reverse, to ask the horse to keep doing what he is doing, move more forward, stop, or slow down. Neutral gear is sitting straight up over your seat bones in a relaxed and balanced position with your center of gravity right over the horse's center of gravity. Neutral gear tells the horse to keep doing what he is doing until you tell him something different. You should ride in neutral almost all the time.

To ask the horse to move forward, inhale. Shift your center slightly forward (a clear signal to the horse to move forward), at the same time allowing your arms to move forward (giving a release to his mouth) and your legs to fall slightly back, closing on the horse's sides and asking him to move forward.

The aids are reversed to ask the horse to stop or slow down: exhale, shift your center of gravity slightly back, while your arms come slightly back and up. Closing the front door for the horse, your legs relax on the horse's sides. As a rider progresses, the leg aids become more articulate to control different parts of the horse's body for turning and for more refined and controlled movements. The rider's hands control the horse from the withers forward, but the legs control the horse's body from the withers back to his tail.

To simplify the use of the leg aids, I teach that there are three leg positions—middle, forward, and back. The middle leg position is when the rider's leg hangs straight down, close to the horse's sides, in the balanced position with ear-shoulder-hip and heel in alignment. Light pressure with one leg on the horse's side from the middle leg position will cause the horse to move his rib cage away from the pressure. This would be useful when asking the horse to arc his body and bend in a circle; as the rib cage moves out, the shoulder and hip bend into the circle.

The forward leg position is applied by reaching toward the girth with your calf. I find it easiest to apply forward leg cues by twisting my lower leg and allowing my heel to come toward the girth or cinch. Pressure from one leg at the forward position will move the horse's shoulder away from the pressure or ask him to bend in the shoulder. When horses turn, they prefer to lean into the turn like a bicycle, thus dropping the shoulder and lurching onto the forehand. Light pressure with the forward leg position will ask the horse to keep his shoulder up and bend properly in the turn.

The back leg aid is applied when the rider's leg shifts back a few inches behind the middle position, and it will ask the horse to move his hip away from the pressure, like you would do for a turn on the forehand. This leg aid might also be used in turning and bending the horse, to keep his hip in toward the center of the circle in order to be properly bent.

Leg aids work together but the rider might be using each leg in a separate position. For instance, if you are using the forward leg position with your inside leg to achieve an arcing turn, your outside leg would be in the back position to also keep the horse's hip in place.

An ancient saying in horsemanship is that the inside leg gives impulsion and the outside leg gives direction. In other words, the inside leg is the gas pedal, and the outside leg is the steering wheel. To control the horse's entire body and negotiate around and through obstacles, the rider must be able to control the horse's nose, shoulder, barrel, and hip. While the hands control the horse's nose, the leg and rein aids work together to control the shoulder, barrel, and hip.

Experiment with applying a light pulsating pressure with one leg in either the forward, middle, or back positions and feel how the horse will yield that part of his body to the pressure.

For more answers, visit the Training Library: www. juliegoodnight. com/ traininglibrary

SECTION 2

Training Techniques to
Refine the
Trail Horse

Well Grounded:
A Lesson on Ground Tying

Park your horse in one spot and know that he will stay there.

My friend's horse, Dodger, stands like a statue on command.

A T A 4-H HORSE SHOW, I watched a trail class with a series of complicated tasks. The class was added as an extra event for the day, and many of the riders entered for fun and weren't totally ready for all of the obstacles. It was a great test for horse and rider. The riders had to ride through a "dog leg" pattern, back up through the same pattern, sidepass over a pole, ride up to a mailbox and pick up a slicker, then dismount and show that their horses would stand still, ground tied, while the youths walked all the way around their horses. For most of the obstacles, the riders could hide any little missteps and correct their horse's footing easily. When it came to the ground-tying test, there was no fudging or fixing to please the judges. It was very evident which riders practiced ground tying and which just crossed their fingers and hoped their horse would magically understand that it was time to stand still.

Horses are smart, but they do need repetition and reinforcement to learn a new skill. Make sure you don't wait until you *need* your horse to ground tie out on the trail. You'll need to practice this skill over and over at home—or as you take a break during long rides. When you're on the trail, ground tying will come in handy if you need to hop down to help doctor a friend's horse, remove debris from the trail, or countless other scenarios. Too often, I've seen the same hoping and praying on the trail—just like what happened at the youth horse show. Hoping that your horse will stand still just because others that you ride with have horses that will ground tie isn't a good idea. On the trail, your horse isn't confined; if he doesn't know that whoa means whoa, you'll set yourself up for an interesting chase. Opt to teach your horse the skills he needs—instead of buying running-shoe inserts for your boots!

Whether you're on your horse's back or dismounted to clear a path, check a hoof, grab lunch, or help a trail buddy, it's important that your horse knows he must follow your directions. If you ask him to stand still, he should stay put without continuous prompting, whether you are on or off him. To accomplish this goal, teach your horse to *ground tie* (stand still, even when you walk away).

By teaching your horse to stand still, you'll help him focus on you and establish yourself as his leader, fulfilling his natural instinct to follow a dominant personality in a herd. You'll teach your horse that you're the trusted leader in your herd of two.

Before mounting up for a long adventure, make sure your horse listens to you when you're on the ground. This may require doing some "homework," and establishing a better relationship and greater authority over your horse by doing groundwork. I've worked hard to create great resources—on DVDs and in articles—to help you make sure you have all the basics of

groundwork and horsemanship in place before you ride. When you are in the saddle, at no point should your horse make his own decisions about what to watch or where to go. You're in charge of his every step, or, in the case of ground tying, his every stance.

Ground tying is a wonderful skill for any horse to have, especially when you are out on the trail and dealing with unknown and some-

Well Grounded

Horsemanship lesson: Teach your horse to stand still on command and not to go anywhere after you have parked him.

Why you need it on the trail: This skill comes in handy anytime you need to hop off to remove fallen branches, open a difficult gate, arrange your saddlebags, help a friend, or simply stop to rest. Teaching ground tying also boosts your confidence in your horse and his confidence that you're in charge, no matter what spooky or interesting conditions surround him.

What you'll do: You'll ask your horse to stand still, vigilantly correcting him by shaking a rope training lead toward his halter anytime he starts to take a step. You'll gradually progress to laying down the rope and walking a short distance away. Finally, you'll test his ground-tying skills by working with him in his usual tack and then you'll be ready to test him out on the trail.

What you'll need: A rope halter; a 12- or 15-foot training lead with a knot attachment to the halter (rather than a metal buckle); your usual bridle with split or loop reins; and your saddle. *Caution:* Never allow loop reins to hang down where your horse can step through them; place them over his head and secure them in a way that removes them from stepping range.

times unforeseeable circumstances. Not only is it convenient when you need to step away from your horse to perform a task, but it's a sure sign that your horse is obedient, focused on you, willing to go with you anywhere (and stay with you anywhere), and trusts your authority and leadership. This kind of rewarding relationship with your horse can only be achieved by investing time in groundwork exercises at home.

Step 1.
Teach Your Horse to Stand Still

Outfit your horse in the rope halter and lead. The long lead will allow you to move farther from your horse as you progress in training–so that gradually your horse is less reliant on your physical presence, but will continue to stand still.

Ask your horse to stand squarely on an even surface. When he stands squarely with all four feet balanced underneath him, he'll be less likely to take a step to maintain his balance (any whisper of a step he takes will earn a correction from you). In addition to not moving his feet, you should also expect him to keep his nose

in front of him and not be looking around for trouble (or for somewhere to go).

Loosely hold the training lead, and stand well in front and slightly to the side of your horse; point your toes toward his shoulder. Don't stand directly in front of your horse; you don't want to be in his path if he spooks and moves forward quickly.

Note: Always face your horse when you want him to stand still; it's easy for him to understand and he'll learn that's a cue. When you want him to move, you'll face the direction in which you wish to go.

Give your horse a verbal "whoa" cue, then watch vigilantly for any movement. The instant he starts to pick up a hoof or moves his nose beyond the width of his shoulders (Photo 1A), issue a correction by snapping the rope.

Correction technique: Flick your wrist up and down to send a wave through the lead toward your horse (be careful not to jerk the lead toward you, which would cue him to move). This wave movement causes the halter-to-lead knot to bump your horse in the chin, letting him know what he was doing at the time was wrong (Photo

Step 1: Stand Still

Step 2: Lay Down the Lead

1B). I prefer to use a lead rope that ties or loops on the rope halter, since the metal buckle hitting his chin may frighten him and besides, buckles are prone to break at the worst possible time out on the trail. The knot is plenty of pressure; a metal attachment can bump your horse in the chin and make him fearful of future corrections.

Important: When your horse moves, correct him immediately. He must receive a correction within three seconds of his infraction to understand your meaning; the sooner within the three-second time frame the correction occurs, the more likely he is to understand. You must use enough pressure to cause a "what-was-that-for?" reaction in your horse. Find the right amount of pressure that motivates the horse to look for the right answer.

Continue working with your horse in this manner until he'll stand still several minutes without a correction and is starting to think first before he moves. Work up to 10 or 15 minutes. Practice this stage daily until your horse stands perfectly still without correction, keeping his attention focused on you, his herd leader.

Gradually stand farther and farther away from your horse, until you reach the end of the long lead. When he stands still at the end of the lead, begin moving from side to side, one step at a time, so that he learns to stand still even when you're moving. Help him know what to do by using your voice cue (whoa) and even giving him a hand signal (like you would when you ask a dog to "stay") if he thinks about moving or looks at you, wondering what he should do.

Practice the standstill in locations around your barn, gradually getting farther away from his comfort zone. Find times to practice when you're sure your horse doesn't want to stand still, such as when the other horses are going back to the barn or he's excited or distracted.

Step 2.
Lay Down the Lead

Once your horse respects your leadership, it's time to test his stick-to-itiveness. When your horse is thinking and understanding, you should begin laying the middle of the lead rope on the ground, with the rope under his nose hanging straight down underneath him and not sloping toward you (which can feel to your horse like pressure to move forward). Although you are still holding the end of the lead and so can make a timely correction by simply picking up the rope, laying it on the ground creates a disconnect between you and your horse. This way, he will begin to learn that when the rope (or later the reins) are laid down, that means don't move!

Ask him to stand squarely. Lay down the lead, and hold onto the very end. Verbally tell your horse "whoa." *Note:* Make sure the lead hangs straight down from your horse's head, so the weight of the rope doesn't pull on his halter, cueing him to move forward.

If your horse turns his head too far (Photo 2) or threatens to take a step, send a large wave through the lead to correct him. You'll need to exaggerate your movement to send the correction through the longer lead length. If your correction is meaningful, he should back

up a step and look concerned about getting in trouble. If he doesn't, you haven't used enough pressure in your correction to motivate him to change his behavior.

Practice with the lead in this position until you can step from side to side around your horse—as far as you can go without dropping the lead—without him moving, and with you rarely having to correct him. This only comes with practice and if you are still making a lot of corrections, go back to the beginning steps and consider that you may not be using enough pressure with your corrections to motivate the horse to learn the cue and obey your instructions.

Step 3.
Walk Away

Now it's time to test your horse a bit more. Position the lead so it hangs down from your horse's halter, and lay all the excess on the ground. Slowly walk a few steps away from him, then stop.

Step 3: Walk Away

Step 4: Tack Up

If your horse moves, issue a stern verbal correction ("whoa!"), and move immediately to the lead to correct him. Your verbal cue will keep his attention on his infraction until you have time to pick up the lead. Lead or back your horse to his original location. Make sure you're not letting him creep closer and closer to where he wants to go—the barn or toward his friends. If you do, he may decide that the infraction is worth the correction if he gets to be a little closer to what he wants. Repeat this exercise until he stands still when you walk a few steps away.

When your horse continues to stand still as you walk a few steps away from your in-front stance, then walk farther away. Gradually increase your distance until you can walk all the way around him, pick up all four feet and walk away from him in any direction.

Note: At first, it'll be easier for your horse if you continue to face him as you move around and away from him, but eventually, he should remain standing, regardless of your body position (Photo 3).

Increase the time your horse will stand ground tied by practicing this exercise when you groom him, tack him up, or even bathe him. Test him frequently; look for opportunities to ground tie him, even if only for a minute.

Step 4.
Tack Up

When your horse consistently stands still on command, you can walk around him and away from him, and you rarely have to issue a correction, it's time to try this exercise in your regular tack.

Outfit your horse in his usual bridle and reins; it might be useful to have his rope halter and training lead on underneath the bridle in case you need to make corrections. If you use split reins, allow them to hang down, mimicking the weight and feel of the rope, but keep loop reins securely over his head to avoid entanglement. Ask your horse to stand squarely, say "whoa," and step away (Photo 4A).

If your horse starts to move, say "whoa" sternly, and move immediately toward him to correct his position. If you are using a halter underneath the bridle, you'll correct him with the lead. To correct his position without a halter, don't use the wave technique you used with the lead. Instead, gently pick up the reins, and use them to cue your horse to back up to his starting position. Then, reissue the "whoa" command.

Important: Never use the reins for punishment, whether on the ground or in the saddle. Use bit pressure only for communication. If you use the reins for punishment, it may cause your horse to fear bit pressure, and consequently lose trust in you as his leader.

When your horse is ready, it's time for the ultimate test. Walk all the way around him while

Tied Away

Question: *I've just started working with a 5-year-old horse that's been out with other horses her whole life, and was never halter broke or started under saddle. When I take her out of the pasture to work, she can't seem to figure out how to stand tied by herself without the safety of other horses close by. She pulls back and breaks every lead rope. How can I teach her to stand tied?*

Answer: While you're noticing this behavior the most when it comes to tying, it sounds like there are several lessons your horse needs to learn. She needs to learn independence from the herd, patience, work ethic, and that she won't always get her own way. Horses—just like children—need to learn these fundamental skills about how to get along.

It's best to teach these skills at an early age. It can prove more difficult to teach the skills when the horse is more set in her ways. Imagine a 20-year-old human (the equivalent of your 5-year-old mare) who never had to go to school, study, or do homework. And imagine that the 20-something also didn't have to clean her room, hold a job, fix a

meal, or clean up the dishes. She can be taught to do all of these basic life skills, but it would have been easier to grow up knowing the basic expectations and learning these important skills before this age.

You'll need to start by doing systematic groundwork with your horse—and lots of it! No doubt, just taking her out of her pen and separating her from the herd will cause lots of drama—even if she isn't tied. Before she learns patience and to stand tied, she needs to learn that her focus should always be on you. She must respect you as a leader in the new herd of two—with you as alpha and she as the willing follower. She'll also need to learn that she has to work—even when she doesn't

feel like it. You'll need to build up basic skills and teach her that you're in charge before you expect her to stand tied.

Start with a regimen of round-pen work so your mare learns to focus on you and respect your authority. In the round pen, she'll quickly learn your cues and expectations. She must move forward when asked, change direction when asked, and stop when asked. She'll learn to focus on you instead of searching for her herd. These steps are demonstrated in my "Round Pen Reasoning" DVD.

When your mare is focusing on you, it's time to progress to working with her on a long lead line and with a rope halter. Teach her the skills she'll need to know to stand tied by asking he stands in place, then walk away and out of his sight (Photo 4B). He should trust that you, his herd leader, have placed him in position, and he will stand still until he receives further orders. You'll trust your horse to stay put, and he'll trust that you're firmly in charge and worthy of being the herd leader.

Ground tying is an important and useful tool out on the trail. In my mind, it's one of the minimum requirements of a good trail horse–particularly a lead horse. To have this much authority over your horse is a wonderful thing, but it does not come for free–you'll have to practice, be consistent in your handling and corrections, and work to maintain this skill in your horse.

---

her to stand still as you hold the lead rope. If she moves a foot or even looks away, correct her by sending a wave through the long training lead. You'll also need to teach her to move forward and turn on command— never getting in front of you or pushing into your space.

The more groundwork you do with your horse, the more she'll learn to focus on you for guidance and leadership. She'll also learn to trust you and look to you for comfort— just as she used to look for comfort from the herd. That skill will be important as you work toward tying her and expecting her to stand still and compliant without other horses around. You can learn more precise steps in the round pen and lead line process at www.juliegoodnight.com/traininglibrary.

After your horse develops a work ethic through groundwork, it's time to start tying her—as often as possible and for long periods of time. I prefer to use a rope halter and strong lead that has a tied-on connection instead of a snap—which can easily break. Look for halters and leads made of high quality, high-tensile marine rope. Tie your mare to a post that's anchored firmly in the ground and will not break (never tie to fence rails or corral panels

since they can break, bend, or move easily). Use a quick-release knot and don't use cross ties. It's a good idea to put rubber mats down so that if she paws or frets too much she'll not dig a deep hole.

Using inferior equipment may result in her learning she can get away if she tries hard enough. Every time she has thrown a fit and broken something (and therefore gotten an immediate release), she has been trained to pull back and not to stand tied.

Now it's time to tie her often when you're around the barn to supervise. For generations, horsemen have called this "time at the patience post." She may need to spend many hours tied before she learns to stand quietly and patiently—especially given that she has broken gear and gotten away in the past.

In the beginning, she'll fuss a lot. Only untie her and return her to her pen when she's standing quietly. As long as she doesn't get a reward for her bad behavior, she'll eventually give it up. It may take a while— she probably would've learned the lesson more quickly as a 2-year-old, but with patience, she can learn now.

More thoughts on pulling back: Some horses pull back when tied out of sheer panic from the

confinement they feel if their flight response is triggered when tied. This is a different case from the "obstinate puller," which is the category I think your horse falls into, from your description. An obstinate puller is usually throwing a tantrum because she doesn't want to be there and the behavior is engrained when the horse breaks something and gets what she wants. A panic puller could be very broke and well mannered and may stand tied for weeks on end just fine until something happens to startle him (usually from a person reaching for his head unexpectedly), then he panics and pulls back. You will see sheer panic in the horse and he may even fall down in a seemingly catatonic state. An unbreakable rope halter will help cure an obstinate puller (because it's too uncomfortable when he pulls back), but it may make a panic puller worse, because of the additional pressure he feels when he pulls back. If you think your horse is pulling because he's panicked, opt for a tying device that allows the horse to pull the rope slightly without breaking free!

For more answers, visit the Training Library: www. juliegoodnight. com/ traininglibrary

Stand for It:
Teach Your Horse to Stand Still While You Mount

Teach your horse to be mannerly and obedient, so he'll stand still and allow you to mount easily, even on the trail.

Tequelo, a model horse on the trail, shows he can stand still and wait for a cue to step off.

OUNTING IN MOTION IS *NOT* my idea of fun. The problem is so common—I see the dancing, hopping, stepping, sidestepping process at most every clinic I teach. I've learned that often the horses that move while you mount think that they're doing the right thing. They've technically been trained to walk off. I believe they actually think that they're helping you get where you're going a little more quickly when they step off sooner and sooner. If you walk or trot off as soon as your bum hits the saddle, your horse soon associates your seat with movement. Then he notices that you always put your foot in the stirrup before you sit—so he can help out and get moving even sooner once he knows that cue. Then the "training" process continues and your horse thinks that if you split the reins, time to walk off is coming. If you don't do something to stop the process, you are training your horse to walk off every time you step near him.

This frustrating cycle can be stopped and even older horses that have been trained to walk off early for years and years can learn a new skill. In one of my favorite "Horse Master" episodes, "Stand By Me," (during the shoot where I first met Shawntel, who now helps on our behind-the-scenes crew), I worked with an 18-year-old Morgan/Quarter Horse mare that had been used all her life as a cow pony and trail guide horse. She was a really sweet mare with the aggravating habit of walking off while you mount. She clearly thought this was the right thing to do. I showed her new owner a simple exercise that would teach the horse to stand. Surprisingly, the mare totally got it the very first time I did the exercise. Thankfully, the cameras were rolling and we didn't have to shoot a second take. We couldn't get the mare to misbehave a second time. I won't guarantee that your horse will learn on the very first try, but it won't take long to teach him how to stand still while you mount. Your days of dancing and bouncing around with your foot in the stirrup are about to end!

Teaching your horse to stand still for mounting will boost your safety on the trail and your ability to trust your horse. If you need to mount or dismount in open spaces, your horse may think that your presence and riding gear means it's time to take off, and if there's precarious footing, his unauthorized exit might cause him or you to slip or fall.

I expect all my horses to stand still on a loose rein for mounting and until I give them a cue to move. A horse that stands still while his rider steps up and waits patiently for a cue to walk off shows that he has manners and knows his place in the herd.

This lesson will detail exactly how you can teach all this to your horse and how you can prevent these problems from occurring in the future.

Stand for It

Horsemanship lesson: Teach your horse to stand still as you mount up.

Why you need it on the trail: When you mount up in the open, it's especially important for your horse to wait patiently for your seat to land in the saddle, to find your stirrups, rebalance your saddle, and get situated; he must continue to wait, standing dead-still on a loose rein until you issue a go-forward cue.

What you'll do: You'll prepare your horse for a ride in an enclosed arena, secure the reins, and attach a longe line to the left ring of his bit or to the halter. As you mount in slow motion, you'll watch for your horse to take a step. As soon as he does, you'll step back and make him work by longeing him actively around you so that he'll associate taking a step when you mount with having to do more work. Once your horse is standing still as you step toward him, you'll praise him for his obedience. Finally, you'll test his standing-still skills by mounting up on the trail.

What you'll need: An enclosed arena or large round pen; a long training lead (12 to 15 feet) or longe line. Your horse should be tacked as usual with bridle, saddle, and saddle pad. If you use a snaffle bit, you can attach the longe line directly to the ring of the bit; or you can keep your halter on underneath the bridle, to attach the longe line or training lead (this may be better if your horse does not longe well).

Step 1: Prepare Your Horse

If your horse walks off as you're trying to get on, chances are you've inadvertently taught him this frustrating behavior. If you've ever allowed your horse to start walking without a cue and as soon as your pockets hit the saddle (or when a horse in front of him moves), you've taught him that the cue to walk is you sitting on his back (or he is taking his cue from another horse).

As the habit continues, your horse trains himself to walk as soon as you put a foot in the stirrup, then as soon as you approach with reins in your hand. While he thinks he's perfecting a cue, you get frustrated and feel unsafe because your horse walks away when your foot is stuck in the stirrup.

To fix this mounting-in-motion problem, I'll teach you how to retrain your horse to stand still for mounting. You'll make your horse think that walking off means work, while standing still is easy and worthy of praise. You'll also remind him that you dictate his every step. If you don't cue him to move, even after you mount, he should stand still and wait for orders from you, his herd leader.

Teaching your horse to stand still for mounting will boost your safety on the trail and your ability to trust your horse. If your horse has less

than perfect mounting manners, it's time to correct his bad habits and establish yourself as your horse's leader. As his leader, only you decide when it's time to move. You make all the decisions for your herd of two.

Step 1.
Prepare Your Horse

Outfit your horse in the tack listed in the box on page 61. Clip the longe line to the ring on the left side of the snaffle bit (Photo 1A). Neatly gather the excess longe line and fold it into your left hand, being careful not to make loops with the line. Place the reins over your horse's head or around his neck and secure them to the saddle so they won't come loose and trip your horse as you work (Photo 1B).

Stand your horse square, so his weight is evenly distributed on all four feet and no leg is cocked. Then you won't inadvertently force him to move for balance when you mount. *Note:* You should always make sure the horse is square before you mount so that he can balance your weight without moving. If he isn't standing square when you mount and must take a step for balance, don't penalize him.

Step 2: Mount Up Slowly

Step 2.
Mount Up Slowly

Approach your horse to mount up, but do so in ultra-slow motion (Photo 2A). Pay attention to where you are in the mounting process when your horse begins to walk without being cued. You may find that simply walking to your horse's side prompts him to move. Or, you may find that you can twist your stirrup and raise your leg–or even get your foot in the stirrup–before he takes a step.

As you test your horse, make sure you don't prevent him from moving. Your goal is that he will stand still with no restraint. He'll need

to make the mistake before you can correct it (Photo 2B). The moment your horse takes a step, it's time to make him work.

The *moment* your horse takes a step, take your foot out of the stirrup, step back and feed out some line. As soon as you're in a safe spot, raise your right arm, slap it on your leg, make a "swoosh" sound, stomp your feet, and make your horse move off in a circle around you (Photo 2C). Be quick and assertive about it–your goal is to teach your horse that walking off without a cue is a bad thing and it means hard work for him.

Be firm so your horse associates his movement with having to work hard. Standing still will now

Trail Etiquette

- When riding in a group (two or more), you should be aware when people are mounting or dismounting and always require your horse to stand still as a courtesy to the other riders. If you allow your horse to walk off while someone is in the middle of mounting, it can create difficulties and is inconsiderate.

- When you come to a gate on the trail, one rider will generally take responsibility for opening and closing the gate, which may or may not require dismounting. Be courteous to the gate operator by walking to the other side, then turning your horse around to face the gate and stand quietly while the operator shuts the gate and remounts. If you continue down the trail and your trail buddy is left behind, it could cause problems.

Step 3: Praise Him

Important: Your horse will learn the lesson quickly if your correction is well timed. Horses associate a behavior with the consequence if a correction comes within three seconds of the original act, and the sooner in the three seconds the correction occurs, the more likely the horse will make an association.

Simply put, if you're quick and put your horse to work the instant he steps off, he may learn his lesson on the first try. If you wait too long before asking him to work, he may not associate the correction with his action. Or, worse, think he was supposed to walk off.

be easy and moving will be hard. Ask him to lope 5 to 10 laps around the longe circle each time so he understands he has to work. Longe him long enough so that he wants to stop. You'll see him breathing hard and looking to you for a stop cue.

When your horse wants to stop, say "whoa," and allow him to rest for a moment. Then square him, and repeat the mounting process. Repeat this process until he stands still as you place your foot in the stirrup.

Step 3.
Praise Him

When your horse will stand still as you get a foot in the stirrup, you'll change your training plan. That is, you'll begin praising him for his new stand-still behavior.

When your horse stands still while you step into the stirrup, resist the urge to get all the way on. Instead, step back down, and praise him and step back away from him momentarily.

Step 4: Mount Up

This rewards his good behavior by releasing the pressure you were putting on him by mounting and it gives him a moment to rest.

Continue approaching your horse repeatedly and go through the process of mounting in slow motion–longeing if he moves, rewarding him if he doesn't by stepping away and giving him a moment without pressure. He should get better and better as he figures out the cause and effect and you'll get farther and farther in the mounting process before he thinks about moving.

Approach as if to mount many times, including bouncing in the stirrup and stepping up, bringing your legs parallel until he stands still every time. If he takes a step, make sure you're ready to correct him with the longe line when necessary.

Step 4.
Mount Up

After your horse will stand still when you put a foot in the stirrup, then bounce your weight up and lift your right foot completely off the ground

WITH JULIE

Behavior Changes
Signal a Problem

Question: *We have a behavior problem with my daughter's 7-year-old Quarter Horse mare. We have owned this mare about 2 1/2 years. The mare is very sweet, was well behaved when we first got her, and would do anything my daughter asked her to do. During this past spring, the mare has started stepping away from Michele (my daughter) when she tries to mount her. At a horse show on Sunday, the mare would not even let her tighten the girth when she tried to saddle her. Michele ended up losing her patience and I think made the situation even worse. The look in the mare's eyes was one of fear when Michele got upset with her. We did take her to the horse chiropractor in July and he said the mare's neck was sore. In August, she was tied in a stall at our county fair, and I don't know if the situation at the fair has somehow made her afraid of horse shows. Do you have any other suggestions?*

Answer: The first thing to do when a horse's behavior changes is to rule out any physical problems. Based on what you describe, I would look for saddle-fitting problems. Even if you have not changed saddles, it is possible that the horse may have changed her shape enough to develop a fit problem; the problem may be exacerbated

at mounting, since a lot of torque is placed on the horse's back at that time. There is also an increasing amount of research being done on mares that indicates that at various points during their heat cycles they may experience back pain when under saddle. I would have the mare checked thoroughly by an equine vet and have your saddle fit

checked by the doctor as well.

If you are still having difficulty tightening the cinch, most likely the horse has become "cinchy," which simply means reactive to the cinch or girth. Generally, humans tightening the girth too hard, too fast, induce this problem.

Ruling out any physical problems with her back or saddle

(Photo 4A). Practice stepping up, then placing your right foot back down on the ground. If your horse takes a step, initiate the correction technique outlined in Step 2. If he stands still, step off, praise him, and step away.

When your horse stands still reliably as you step up, it's time to fully mount. Keep in mind that after you swing your leg over his back, you'll use rein pressure to stop him and correct him, if necessary. But up until that point, he should willingly stand still on a loose rein. Any unauthorized movement while you are on the ground or stepping up is corrected by longeing, but once you swing your leg over, you'll take control with your hands.

When your horse stands still as you mount and dismount, practice mounting in an open arena (Photo 4B). As you do, keep the longe line attached in case you need to correct him. Keep in mind that his training is location specific. He may behave perfectly in the arena, but need a refresher course when you're in an open area.

Maintain good mounting manners by requiring your horse to stand patiently after you have mounted, until you give him a specific cue to walk forward. Mounting, then rushing off as soon as you put your foot in the stirrup, is what causes the horse to develop bad mounting manners to begin with. Make sure as you trail ride that your horse doesn't begin walking just because the other horses around him started walking—your horse should wait for a cue from you, his captain.

Behavior Changes (continued)

fit, we must look to a training issue regarding the horse moving away for mounting. It is very common for a horse's training to deteriorate when being handled and ridden by novices, and especially a horse as young as yours. Given that she was less than five when you got her, even though she was very well trained, she was not very seasoned, or experienced. A horse this young is pretty easy to "un-train."

If the horse is not standing for mounting, you need to first work on teaching the horse to stand when you ask her to. Then carry this over to mounting; take it very slowly and correct her when she moves (see this lesson).

Make sure that the horse is standing square when you go to mount, and that there is not excessive torque being put on her back and withers. If you unbalance the horse during mounting, it is hard for her to stand still. If you hang on the horse's sides, it can put excruciating pressure from either side of the saddle tree. If the rider doesn't square the saddle after mounting and before asking the horse to move off, the pressure can lead to serious damage to the horse's back from the rider pulling on or hanging off the saddle.

Finally, it is quite possible that if your horse had a bad experience at a show, then she would have a bad association with shows. I am not sure why being tied in a stall would cause this, but horses are very place-oriented when it comes to the associations they make. In other words, if a horse has an unpleasant, frightening, or painful experience, he will tend to associate the place where it happened with the bad memory. This is why it is extremely important to make sure a horse has a very pleasant experience at his first few shows–even if it means not actually showing the horse, but hauling him to the show to simply let him become accustomed to the environment with as little pressure as possible being put on him. There is also a Q&A on my website, called "Seasoning a Horse for Shows," that will explain this process. There will always be small setbacks in a horse's training and times when we have to back up and iron out the rough spots. In addition to consulting with a veterinarian, you may need to get some help from a trainer or instructor who can take an objective look at what is going on with your mare and help you develop a plan to counteract it.

For more answers, visit the Training Library: www. juliegoodnight. com/ traininglibrary

Jig No More:
Stop Anxious Behavior and Walk on a Loose Rein

Work through your horse's "jiggy" behavior.

I'm riding Slide with a relaxed body position and a loose rein so that he won't become worried and "jig" like the tense, gray horse (inset).

WHEN I HEAR THE WORD "JIGGING," I automatically picture a chicken and an egg. Which came first? A jiggy horse is tense because his rider is tense, and the rider is tense because the horse jigs, and the horse jigs because the rider is pulling on his mouth, and the rider pulls on the reins because the horse seems to want to take off, and the horse wants to take off because he wants to get away from the pressure of the bit on his mouth, and...well, you see...

No horse wants to be jiggy. Actually, most horses would rather relax and not work at all. Have you ever seen a horse jig in the field? No, because they aren't feeling your tension and you aren't there to complete the cycle. I have

yet to encounter a horse that was not responsive to correcting this behavior. Most often, when the horse jigs, the rider picks up on the reins to make him stop, but then does not release the reins (or only releases a tiny bit) when the horse walks. And/or the rider does not trust the horse to walk and so keeps hold of the reins and pretty soon the horse is jigging BECAUSE the rider is holding the reins too tight, and the horse is anxious about his mouth. Also, in anticipation of the jig, the rider is typically perched forward in a tense position, with her center of gravity in front of the horse, and the horse associates this position with trotting.

The solution that I have always had success with is to pick up high on the reins (sitting back on your pockets at the same time) when he breaks into the trot, and the instant the horse walks, drop the reins dramatically to a very loose rein, with your hands actually laying on the horse's neck so he can feel them. He may only walk a step or two before he trots again; then pick up and release dramatically (the rein drop has to be very dramatic so that the horse notices).

Soon he will associate walking with a totally loose rein and that is what he wants (that is what any horse wants). Also, it really helps to concentrate on the walk rhythm, sit down on him solidly, and make sure you are not tensing in your seat in anticipation of the horse breaking into trot. Often in this situation, people tense in their seat thinking that the horse is going to break into a trot and pretty soon, the horse thinks he is supposed to be trotting because he feels the rider's weight shifting forward. So make sure you are sitting well back on your seat bones with loose and relaxed joints, concentrating on the feel of the walk rhythm.

Trust the horse to walk on a loose rein. If you feel him tense up like he might trot, just sit

Jig No More

Horsemanship lesson: You'll learn how to stop your horse's jiggy behavior by stopping him abruptly, and dramatically loosening your reins. The dramatic change will help your horse associate relaxation, and a loose rein, with moving in a flat-footed walk.

Why you need it on the trail: You should be able to relax and enjoy the scenery on the trail. You won't be able to do this if you have to rate your horse's speed with every stride and if you're bouncing down the trail in a springy jog. Plus, if your horse continually jigs, he'll not only be stressed, but also he'll develop musculature that will keep his back arched and his head high.

What you'll do: You'll abruptly stop your jigging horse and immediately loosen the reins. By doing so, you'll show him that stopping and moving correctly should be associated with a loose rein. The release of bit pressure is his reward for doing the right thing.

What you'll need: Your saddled horse and long continuous-loop reins that are easy to collect and handle. In this lesson's photos, I am using reins I designed to be easy to handle; they are 9 feet long from end to end.

Skills your horse will need: Your horse should accept a rider, and respond to a voice, seat, and rein cue to stop.

relaxed. Do not correct him unless he actually breaks into a trot. That way he learns to trust you, too, and he learns that he is only corrected if he actually trots. Don't get sucked into the vicious cycle of you pulling all the time and him jigging all the time. You can make the change!

Is your horse "jiggy" and tense on the trail? Does he trot anxiously in place, refusing to move forward in a relaxed frame? If so, you're likely tense and worried that he'll take off if you don't hold him back with constant rein pressure. He has a high headset and looks as though he could burst forward with catapulting energy—a dangerous scenario on the trail, and an aggravating and uncomfortable ride.

You want your horse to move forward in a relaxed manner, not coiled like a spring, but your horse receives mixed signals, and wants to escape the tension he feels in your body and rein cues. He's learned that tight reins mean he should be worried and anxious. Instead, he must learn what you really want— for him to walk forward on a loose rein with his head down.

In this lesson, I'll teach you how your body and rein cues can send the wrong message to your horse and teach him to be tense. I'll then give you a step-by-step sequence to train your jiggy horse to relax and move forward slowly on a loose rein.

I often see jiggy horses on the trail and in my clinics. Jiggy behavior is the result of a cycle of tension—the horse feels tense and wants to speed up, then the rider feels the horse speed up and becomes tense as she uses her muscles to pull back in an attempt to slow the horse's speed.

The jiggy horse has a tense and worried rider who isn't in control of her horse's speed and direction. If your horse is jiggy, he isn't staying at the speed you want, and becomes too tense and confused to follow your direction.

Note that the jiggy gray horse in the inset photo on page 67 has a high headset and an open mouth, and is ready to jump forward. His rider is pulling back with fairly tight rein aids, and is squeezing with her legs. While she thinks that she's telling the horse to slow down with her rein aids, her tight legs are telling him to zoom ahead. These mixed signals cause him to be anxious and jiggy.

You shouldn't have to constantly rate your horse's speed. If you tell him to pick up a particular gait, he should stay in that gait, at the speed you dictate, until you give a new cue and command.

To help your jiggy horse understand your speed commands, you'll need to teach him a new set of cues. Here's how to teach him to associate slow, relaxed movement with loose reins and your relaxed body position.

Step 1.
Whoa!

Your jiggy horse is so used to your pulling on the reins that he doesn't understand anymore that bit pressure is a cue to stop. To end the jiggy behavior, you'll need to stop in a dramatic and abrupt fashion, using your seat and weight as well as the reins, so that he can feel the difference in your cue and will stop. You'll need to escalate your stop cue so your jiggy horse obeys and listens during his new training session.

To stop with gusto, say "whoa," then sit deep onto your pockets and take up abruptly on the reins. In Photo 1A, I grab both reins in my left hand and anchor my hand into my horse's mane. With my right hand, I pull back even more until my horse stops completely (Photo 1B).

Step 1: Whoa!

Note that my hips are tucked under and my upper body is canted back to give my horse a firm seat and weight aid, in addition to the rein cue. With my long rope reins, I'm able to easily handle the reins and slide my hands into position.

Note that if this "whoa" command isn't more dramatic than your usual slow-down and whoa cues, your horse won't understand that this training session is different—and will continue his jiggy behavior. The command needs to be different and abrupt enough to inspire a complete stop and signal a change to him.

Immediately after your horse stops, be ready for the next step: the dramatic release.

Step 2.
Release and Relax

As soon as you stop, give your horse a quick, dramatic release: immediately relax your body

position, place one hand at the end of the loop reins, and drop your hand down to his neck to show him that he can relax his head.

This release shows your horse that he won't feel pressure from the reins if he's relaxed, so he learns that staying relaxed is the desired behavior. This association teaches him that he'll get the loose rein he craves when he's stopped or moving slowly.

Your horse doesn't want you to pull on the reins. He has also likely learned that when the reins are relaxed, and he feels your knuckles on his neck, it probably means that you're relaxed and taking a break (Photo 2A). He doesn't want to move with tension and doesn't want to work harder than he has to.

As you stand still with your knuckles on your horse's neck, you'll remind your horse of other relaxed times when he didn't have to work. He'll associate your loose rein with

2A

Step 2: Release and Relax

relaxation and will begin to understand that you don't want him to be tense. Stand still, and keep your body relaxed for a few moments. Don't hurry on to the next step.

Step 3.
Walk On

Now it's time to ask your horse to move forward with the same relaxation he feels as he's standing still.

With your reins still long and loose, hold on with two hands, and ask your horse to step forward. To do so, use your usual voice cue; gently close your legs on his side, if necessary, but be very careful not to over-cue your horse—try to use as little pressure as possible, and just ease him forward into a relaxed walk.

Sit back and breathe deeply to show your horse that you're just as relaxed as you were when you were standing still. Concentrate on keeping your weight back and your body moving slowly in the walk rhythm.

If your horse begins to jig or speed up, repeat Steps 1 and 2. Keep repeating these steps

Step 3: Walk On

as necessary. Your goal is to gradually gain more and more calm and relaxed steps before needing to repeat the stop-release-relax-walk process.

It's very easy to fall into the trap of thinking your horse is going to speed up. That causes you to shorten the reins and tense your body in preparation for the trot. Eventually, this becomes an inadvertent cue to the horse when what is really happening is that you think he

is going to trot so you prepare for it, and by preparing for it, you cue your horse to do it. Breaking the habit in your own riding is just as important as retraining the horse. You'll have to really concentrate on sitting back and moving your hips slowly in the walk rhythm.

The truth is that jigging is not comfortable or productive for your horse, either. He'd much prefer to be relaxed and walking on a loose rein. This exercise will teach him what to do to

Q&A WITH JULIE

Social Butterfly

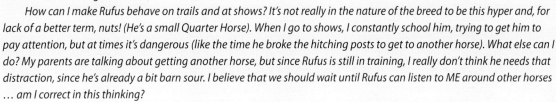

Question: My horse, Rufus (an 8-year-old large pony trained by my 14-year-old self with my trainer), was not trained until he was 6 years old.

Since he was thrown in a field with other horses until he was 6, he is very social. We don't have another horse, but when we go to shows, or I trail ride with my friends, he goes nuts. He won't pay attention to me at all, and is constantly neighing to others, especially mares. (He did try to breed mares in his old field, and he's a gelding. We can't ride him if there's a mare in heat in the area–he goes CRAZY).

How can I make Rufus behave on trails and at shows? It's not really in the nature of the breed to be this hyper and, for lack of a better term, nuts! (He's a small Quarter Horse). When I go to shows, I constantly school him, trying to get him to pay attention, but at times it's dangerous (like the time he broke the hitching posts to get to another horse). What else can I do? My parents are talking about getting another horse, but since Rufus is still in training, I really don't think he needs that distraction, since he's already a bit barn sour. I believe that we should wait until Rufus can listen to ME around other horses … am I correct in this thinking?

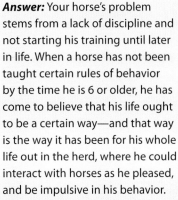

Answer: Your horse's problem stems from a lack of discipline and not starting his training until later in life. When a horse has not been taught certain rules of behavior by the time he is 6 or older, he has come to believe that his life ought to be a certain way—and that way is the way it has been for his whole life out in the herd, where he could interact with horses as he pleased, and be impulsive in his behavior.

The solution to this bad behavior is groundwork, so that your horse learns that you are in fact in charge of every movement and action he makes. My video series on groundwork explains this process in great detail and gives you specific exercises to do to help build a solid relationship with your horse and teach him ground manners. Through groundwork, a horse learns that you are in charge, you make the decisions, and you dictate the actions he makes—you become his central focus, rather than all the other horses. Horses must learn that when they are

around humans, there are certain rules that must be followed, just like there are expected rules of behavior out in the herd.

There are many articles in my Training Library about doing groundwork with horses to teach ground manners, obedience, and fundamental rules of behavior, and to develop the leader-follower relationship with your horse. The most important thing you need to work on with your horse is getting control of his nose. If you can control his nose, both from the ground and from the saddle, you can prevent the problems you are having. Read up on nose control from the Training Library on my website and get some help doing groundwork with your horse.

Horses must learn at some age (the sooner, the better) that they cannot act out their impulsive herd behaviors when they are in a working situation or around humans. Even a stallion that is bred a lot can easily learn when that behavior is acceptable and when it is not.

Never let your horse fraternize or interact with other horses when you are handling him or riding him. This just should not be allowed; it is not safe and it is not good for herd health, when the horses are from different herds.

In situations like you describe, it is best to use the training theory known as "replacement training." This means that when a horse displays an undesirable behavior, rather than punish the bad behavior, you would replace it with another more desirable behavior. In the instance of your horse losing his focus, it might help to put him to work doing something else. I would start immediately working the horse, not in a harsh, quick or punishing way, but just making him do something that would probably involve changing directions again and again. So I might put him to the trot, ask him to turn right, then go straight, then go left, then go straight, then go right, etc. Throw in some transitions (changes of speed get the loose rein—but only if you re-program your own riding, too. Do not tolerate the jig—stop him abruptly, then re-cue him for a slow walk, but then trust him to walk out on a loose rein. Correct him abruptly when he makes a mistake by breaking into the jig. If you try to hold him in the walk, it will only encourage his jigging. If you show him that walking calmly gets him what he wants—a loose rein, he'll gladly do it!

You'll break the cycle of tension and clearly show your horse that you're the leader of the herd. You're the one deciding that the herd will be relaxed and move ahead slowly.

Social Butterfly (continued)

or gait), so the horse has to listen to you. When the horse focuses on you, let him rest, but away from the other horses. Do not let him come back to the "herd" until he is quiet, obedient, and relaxed. Take him away and put him to work as soon as he becomes distracted again.

From the incidents you describe, and the herd-bound behavior you are dealing with, it sounds like your horse is emotionally needy. His herd-bound behavior will only get worse as he ages if you don't get and keep a handle on it. Find opportunities to keep him by himself—tied at the trailer alone, in a turnout pen by himself, riding by yourself, etc. This will help him gain independence and also make him more eager to be around you for company.

When you are handling him—whether riding or doing groundwork—his focus should be totally on you. If he looks around or is noncompliant, put him to work, take command, get inside his mind, and draw his focus back to you. Start with this process while you are riding alone, and then insist on the same level of obedience when you are with others. With a real needy

or really herd-bound horse, I would have a zero-tolerance policy—focus stays on me at all times.

Examine your relationship with this horse. Chances are there are little things you are doing—which you may not even be aware of— that are eroding your authority with him. He needs stronger leadership from you. Does he ever control your actions? Does he invade your space at times, eat grass while you are leading him, ignore your cues? Does he go exactly where you point him and maintain a steady speed that you dictate when you are riding? Has he trained you to feed him treats? If you examine it closely, you'll probably find some holes in your authority that are eroding your horse's confidence in your leadership ability.

I've said this many times before—there's only one conversation to have with your horse and it goes like this: "Horse, this is your captain speaking." Everything else that follows is a direct order. The horse is your first mate and his job is to carry out your orders—not to ignore orders, suggest alternatives, or argue about your decision. If he's a good first mate, he will be

the apple of the captain's eye and have many privileges, but if he's not, he'll be fired and made to walk the plank. This is the kind of relationship your horse knows and seeks—acceptance into the herd of a strong and fair leader, and the threat of banishment if he cannot abide by the rules. When he accepts you as that strong and benevolent leader, then the other horses won't matter so much to him.

I think that if you invest some time in groundwork so that you learn to control your horse's nose, feet, shoulder, and hip, and you gain control over his impulsive actions, you will no longer have the problems you describe. However, I am not disagreeing with your parents, as far as you getting another horse. If you were my daughter, I would prefer that you have a well-trained, obedient, and therefore safer horse that was ready for you to go out and enjoy and help you accomplish your personal competitive goals.

For more answers, visit the Training Library: www. juliegoodnight. com/ traininglibrary

Fear Not:
Reprogram Your Spooky Horse

Learn to guide your horse past potentially spooky objects with this lesson. Here Tequelo learns to walk over the bridge without a spook.

Train your horse to face his fears.

HORSES ARE, FIRST AND FOREMOST, flight animals by nature. Their strong propensity toward flight, combined with their prey mentality, can be a powerful thing to control, especially when riding in unfamiliar terrain.

Whether your trail riding takes you to the top of tall mountains, through dark woods, across open desert or into urban wilderness, your horse may occasionally encounter spook-worthy stimuli. How he learns to handle himself in these situations can make the difference between a momentary pause in your ride or a dramatic spin and bolt, ending with you sitting in the dirt with a long walk home ahead of you.

Some horses will spook at their own shadow, while others rarely shy from anything. Many horses are "bombproof" in familiar terrain but fall apart in new or strange environs. If your horse is prone to fearful behavior, you'll definitely want to spend some time actively de-spooking him, replacing his natural tendency to spin and bolt with stopping, facing, and approaching what he is afraid of. Even if you are blessed with a brave horse, you may occasionally encounter a spooky stimulus and this de-spooking process will come in handy.

While a horse's natural instinct is to spin and bolt away from anything that scares him, a horse is also instinctively curious—the behaviorists call this "investigative behavior." The key to de-spooking a horse is to teach him that first, flight is not an option and you must face what you're afraid of. The next step is to promote his investigative behavior and thus, diffuse his fear.

As his confidence builds, so will yours. If your horse is so spooky that you are not confident in the saddle, you can start doing these exercises from the ground with your horse by setting up novel challenges in your barnyard. Or you can take the same training plan to the saddle and go through the process with you on his back. Making a plan, taking action, and putting your mind and energy into training your

Fear Not

Horsemanship lesson: Teach your horse to approach and accept any scary object.

Why you need it on the trail: Even the most benign trail ride can present perceived threats in your horse's mind. You need to know how to keep him from spooking and bolting—potentially unseating you and causing injury.

What you'll do: As you ride, you'll keep your horse focused on the scary object, turning toward the stimulus and stopping him from turning to bolt. You'll take a deep breath, maintain visual and mindful focus, be calm and relaxed, and avoid prompting your horse to become even more fearful. You'll make sure he remains obedient as you ask him to stop and look toward the scary object. Your goal is to prevent his flight response from triggering while encouraging his curiosity.

What you'll need: Your usual tack, a helmet, and an object or situation that's new to your horse. If you plan to start from the ground, use a rope halter and long training lead, and you may want to have him saddled so he is in a riding frame of mind. Set up an obstacle that your horse hasn't seen before, or recreate a situation that has spooked your horse on the trail. If your horse is typically "bombproof," test his willingness to approach something that moves or makes an unusual sound, such as a plastic bag caught in a tree. In the following photos, I added a potted plant to my horse's familiar bridge crossing. This seemingly small addition caused my horse to rethink an obstacle he'd approached many times before.

Note: If you don't feel safe or comfortable with your horse, or if your horse is young and inexperienced, ask an experienced horseperson or trainer to help you through your horse's desensitizing process.

Warm-up exercise: Mount up, and warm up your horse as usual, well away from the new obstacle. Perform small circles to the right and left. If you are working from the ground first, do some lead line work away from the challenges you have set up so you start off on the right foot with your horse. Make sure you can calmly turn him in both directions and that he's listening to your turn cues to stop, go, and turn.

horse are achievements that will not only help your horse, but will build your confidence, too. Having a plan of action also keeps your mind from becoming polluted with thoughts of fear. There are a lot of actions you can take to resolve the issues surrounding fearful behavior in your horse and yourself. Now it's up to you.

As a trail rider, you likely encounter any number of spooky obstacles and scary objects. Can you count on your horse to quietly and willingly approach such obstacles without spooking? Do you have a plan in place to help introduce him to new challenges?

Because horses are prey animals, they're hardwired to be on the alert, looking for any sign of an attack and preparing to bolt. They easily sense changes in the environment and notice movements, sounds, and smells that people have learned to disregard. Their eyes and brain are programmed to notice sudden movements that may signal a predator that lies still in the grass before pouncing.

You may have noticed that your horse is much edgier than usual on a windy day. That's because his senses are overwhelmed from the environment—everything is moving, it's too noisy to hear, too windy to smell. From your horse's point of view, it is best to be on high alert during these times and instinctively, he may think that it is best to react first and ask questions later.

Or, you may have a horse who is great on the trail from your barn that you have ridden a thousand times, but when you ride a new trail he spooks at everything. Or maybe he's fine with a group of horses, but a total fraidy cat by himself. You, however, would probably like to ride a calm, relaxed trail mount—no matter what the environmental conditions or situation.

While some horses are spookier than others, all horses can react to unusual sights, sounds, sensations, and smells. The good news is that any horse can be desensitized and taught to approach any fear-inducing obstacle.

Horses have a unique ability to transition from fearful and spooky to trusting and willing if they have a confident leader. Here, I'll teach you how to help your horse through a spook and help him confidently approach any object. You'll practice these techniques at home, then apply those skills on the trail.

Horses rely on all of their senses to identify a potential threat. Your horse might react to an unusual odor (that you might not smell), a strange sound (soft or loud), or an unaccustomed sensation (such as a branch scraping his side). Even the most predictable trail horse can spook at a new scenario or a combination of stimuli.

While horses easily settle into a routine, they'll notice if something is suddenly different and they'll become suspicious. For instance, if a horse passes a mailbox every day as he leaves the property, he may suddenly spook if the mailbox flag is up. He may see the mailbox as a new monster, capable of attack—until it's proven otherwise.

When your horse spooks, he probably *balks* (stops suddenly on the forehand), then spins, rears, and/or leaps. These extreme reactions can unseat even a seasoned rider.

After the initial spook, your horse may also bolt. That's because when he turns his nose away from the scary object, his flight response kicks in. At that point, he may run an eighth of a mile or more before stopping to consider just what it is he's running away from. This is a react-first, think-later behavior, which is instinctive to the horse.

Step 1: Control His Nose

I will teach you how to avoid the bolt, and how to keep your horse's nose pointed at the object that spooks him. Instead of allowing his flight response to kick in, you'll help him stay present and start thinking, invoking another natural response: curiosity.

Step 1.
Control His Nose

Guide your horse toward the obstacle at a walk. Start at least 20 yards away to give him a chance to notice a change in his usual environment. Approaching from a distance will also allow you to notice small changes in his body language and alertness, so you can control his movements before he can manage a dramatic spook, turn, and bolt.

At the first sign of tension in your horse's body—perking his ears, tensing his muscles or leaning away from the obstacle (Photo 1A)—calmly ask him to stop but make sure you keep his nose pointed directly at the object. At this point, you should be riding two-handed. Don't

allow him to move backward, left, or right. Standing still and focusing on the object that caused concern is the only option.

When you ask your horse to stop, it keeps him obedient and responsive to your cues, and gives you a reason to praise him. Stopping and standing gives him a moment to observe the new object, take a deep breath, and relax. Make sure you do the same—you can trigger your horse to relax by taking a deep breath yourself.

If your horse tries to turn away—if he even starts to look slightly to one side or the other—correct his focus by picking up on the opposite rein and pointing his nose back to the obstacle or just bumping the lead line if you are working from the ground.

If your horse turns his head to the right, bump the left rein, and vice versa. Use the amount of rein pressure needed to get an immediate response. Don't allow him to refuse your turn cue or turn the way he'd like. He must learn that turning away (and therefore invoking his flight response) isn't an option (Photo 1B).

Here, my horse looks to the left, planning a turn. Notice that my arms are in front of me, encouraging my horse not to back away as I correct his nose position, turn him back to the right, and point him straight toward the scary plant.

At this point, you're not asking him to approach the object. You're asking him only to stop moving forward, backward, left, or right, and look at the object that causes him tension or fear. Soon, he'll understand that there's no option for leaving and he can easily stand still and face what he's afraid of. Reward him when he shows interest in the scary thing.

As soon as your horse stops trying to turn away from the scary object, loosen the reins, take a deep breath (to signal your non-concern), and rub him on the neck to praise him for being obedient.

Step 2.
Take a Forward Step

Ask your horse to take a step or two—but no more—closer to the object (Photo 2A). Just as in Step 1, you'll keep his nose pointed toward the obstacle and keep your own focus on where you want to go. After he's moved a step or two closer to the object, say "whoa," as you gently sit back and stop him, making sure his nose stays pointed toward the object.

Again, loosen the reins, take a deep breath and rub your horse on the neck to praise him for responding to your commands (Photo 2B). Make sure to *rub* your horse on the neck—which signals him to relax—instead of patting him. Patting can energize and stimulate instead of relax your horse.

Ask your horse to step forward, then stop, and do this several times until you get closer and closer to the object. Always stop after a few steps, praise him, and encourage him to relax. With each repetition, he'll gain confidence, and his initial fearfulness of the object will dissipate. He'll get used to seeing, hearing, smelling, and sensing the object. He'll understand that you, his herd leader, are encouraging him and praising

Step 2: Take a Forward Step

Step 3: Encourage Curiosity

him for his approach, and he'll remain in an obedient frame of mind as he responds to your stop and go cues.

Step 3.
Encourage Curiosity

Asking your horse to stop moving toward the scary object not only helps him relax, but helps him become curious about the item in front of him. Although curiosity, or investigative behavior, is instinctive in the horse, it will only kick in once flight is ruled out.

Imagine telling a young child not to look in the hall closet the day before her birthday. You'll inspire her curiosity and may prompt her to snoop for presents. The same idea applies to your horse regarding the once-scary object. As soon as you ask him to stop and look at the item, he'll become curious about it. His fear will convert to curiosity, and you'll feel him become drawn to the object, like a magnet.

When your horse anticipates your go-

forward cue and seems to want to go forward, allow his forward motion for a few steps.

Here, my horse willingly stepped forward and put his nose on the potted plant (Photo 3A).

When your horse steps forward, loosen the reins, and allow the forward motion, and give him praise and affirmation for his curiosity (Photo 3B). But then hold him back a little so he becomes even more curious about the object. Asking him to stop after a few steps will have the same effect as telling your child not to look in the closet—his curiosity will grow even stronger.

Make a game out of this exercise that your horse will love to play. When he approaches the object and touches it with his muzzle, declare him the winner—with copious praise.

When you've made sure your horse's curiosity results in relaxation instead of another spook, ask him to move forward and past the object that first caused him fear. With practice, frequent stops, and praise, he'll soon approach whatever you place in his path.

Unfocused and Confused

Question: *I have a 10-year-old horse who was born on my farm. From day one, he has been an ADD/spooky horse. He has been a challenge and although we have made progress, I'm always back to square one. I have done so much with him–my background is in dressage, but I do a lot of groundwork, some round-pen work, longeing–I take him places, to clinics and shows now and then–but I still struggle with getting his attention. Is it possible that he doesn't like ring work? He does like trail riding with his buddies, but is still spooky and inattentive most days. Once in a while he's kind of relaxed. Progress is very slow.*

Answer: It sounds like you have already tried a lot of different things with this horse with some success, but the progress has been slow. At 10 years old, he ought to be getting pretty mature and reliable, especially with all the work you have done. I would like to have an opportunity to see your horse and work with him a little, but in lieu of that, here are a few things I might try with a horse like this.

I like to teach spooky horses to face their fear and—as long as they face it—they can stop and relax, with lots of reassurance from me. So the first cardinal rule is that when the horse stops and faces what he is afraid of (instead of spinning and bolting), he gets a reward. He gets a rub on the neck and gets to stop and relax. Then I will gently encourage him to move toward whatever he is afraid of; I ask him to move forward one step at a time, stopping him with each step (so that I remain in control, issuing the orders), and rewarding him. This eventually becomes a game to the horse and he loves to work for the reward. He gets the ultimate reward when he will actually walk all the way up to the scary object and reach out and touch it with his nose. You can

practice this on the ground, too.

One big problem with horses like you describe is that they do not focus on you and do not look to you for leadership. This kind of relationship (focused and obedient) is best accomplished with groundwork, both lead line and round pen. It sounds like you have done a lot of this already, but in my experience, I have seen a lot of people do the groundwork but without succeeding in getting the horse's total focus. For instance, the horse may run well around the round pen and do turns and stops, etc., but if his total focus is not on you almost all the time, then the round-pen work may have been meaningless chasing of the horse.

After the horse is moving away from me well in the round pen and I can control which direction he goes, then I want to establish a line of communication with him so that he is constantly looking to me for directives. If his focus wanders outside the round pen, then I put him to work. Not harshly, and not chasing him, but asking him to do something like go faster, go slower, turn this way, turn that way, etc. When his focus is on me because he has to see what I am going to ask him to do next, I let him stop and relax. This same

concept can be applied for lead line work and mounted work. Just be careful that when you ask the horse for more focus, you are not getting fast and reactive to him and escalating his tension, but are just quietly issuing directives to the horse and reinforcing what you ask of him. It is very important that you have and keep control of the horse's nose, both on the ground and especially in the saddle. Most people let their horse's nose wander all over the place and look at whatever interests them. This is a root cause of many behavioral and obedience problems. Usually, the very first indication that a horse is thinking about doing something he shouldn't is when the nose leaves its position from in front of his chest. We work very hard with our colts and any older horses that come for training with behavior problems to teach this very, very important rule, "Thou shalt keep your nose directly in front of your chest at all times that I am working around you or riding you." If you set this very simple rule with your horse and then enforce it 100 percent of the time, within minutes, your horse will become obedient.

I think it is important to master this rule on the ground first, but I

Unfocused and Confused *(continued)*

also work on it while riding. From the ground, all you have to do is ask the horse to stand (that is another very important ground rule we set right away, "Thou shalt not move thy feet unless I tell you to move them"), and then step back away from the horse. He should stand there of his own volition, not because you have a choke hold on the halter rope. Correct his nose with a gentle bump of the halter rope every time he moves his nose away from you and point at his nose or twirl the tail of the rope toward his nose every time he moves the nose toward you. Just put his nose back where you told it to stay every time it moves; be slow and calm with your corrections but always consistent and firm when necessary. If he moves his feet when you correct his nose, put him back where he was and tell him whoa (standing still is another rule that must be reinforced in the same way). Work on nose control standing in an open area for 5 to 10 minutes and the horse will learn his boundaries. Then I want to reinforce this rule at the hitching rail and at all times when I am working around the horse.

When a horse moves his nose toward you, unasked, that is an invasion of your space, and an indication that the horse does not respect your space (often because he has been hand-fed treats and this has caused major disrespect; see the article on my website called "Trick or Treat"). So moving his nose toward me is a greater infraction than moving his nose away. Depending on the horse, that might get a harsher correction from me, especially if it is a horse that

has proven his lack of respect by walking all over me or ignoring me or even being aggressive.

Carrying over this rule (nose control) to the saddle is very important for a spooky horse. When he learns to obey this rule, he will not really be able to spook and his focus will remain on you. He can pick his head up and look at anything he wants to, as long as his nose stays in front of his chest. If it moves to either side, I will correct it with a gentle and slow bump of one rein (if he is turning his nose to the right, use the left rein and vice versa).

Again, it is not a pull or a jerk, but a slow gentle bump up on the rein. I will keep bumping (not pulling) until the nose comes back to center. If you set this rule and then enforce it, in short order the horse will learn to keep his nose centered. He may still make the occasional mistake and you will have to correct him consistently for some time.

One common scenario I see in horses like you describe is a co-dependent relationship with the rider. It goes something like this: the horse is spooky or fractious and the rider gets uptight, and since horses reflect our own emotions, the tension escalates on both sides. Then the rider, knowing the horse is going to do it again, keeps a tense and tight hold on the reins and begins to look for the next spooky object, telegraphing to the horse, "I don't trust you, and there must be something out there to be afraid of." Again, horses reflect our emotions, so the horse becomes more tense and irritated from the rein pressure, causing an escalation in the rider's tension that leads to irritation and anger in the rider. So

now the rider is getting mad and frustrated at the horse and jerking and hitting, instead of using calm and consistent correction, and the horse, again reflecting our emotions, gets frustrated and mad, too. This is a terrible dynamic that can go on for days, weeks, months, or years but at some point, either the horse or the rider will reach the boiling-over point and a major problem may ensue.

This negative dynamic must be stopped at some point—the sooner, the better. When a rider is resentful, angry, or emotional toward the horse, the horse is typically reflecting those same emotions right back at the rider. This is a negative situation that has little chance for success. At this point, it is important to look for a way to change the dynamic and do something different. Often, the rider needs to take a deep breath, summon up some patience, and most importantly, relax and SLOW DOWN corrections and communications to the horse. Hopefully you and your horse have not yet fallen into this trap and some of these things may help you break the dynamic. If I can teach the horse to respond to some basic rules, and he can trust that I will enforce the rules, his life becomes more predictable and safe. He will relax and know that, as long as he follows the rules, everything is good and his focus will be on me as his leader. Good luck with this horse and I hope I get the opportunity to work with you both in person sometime.

For more answers, visit the Training Library: www. juliegoodnight. com/ traininglibrary

Take the Plunge:
Cross Water with Confidence

Learn how to safely introduce your horse to water crossings.

Here, I'm on a young, inexperienced Quarter Horse filly to show that water crossings can be easy and safe.

REMEMBER THE ADAGE "NEVER SAY NEVER" when it comes to horses? Well, when it comes to taping our TV show, "Horse Master," we've struck out three times in a row on water-crossing episodes—in each case, the so-called "problem horse" turned out to be just fine with water as soon as the camera turned on. The last one was a really cute Morgan gelding, and although he did not walk right into the water, it didn't take much to get him there. The actual "problem" was a rider who made the mistake of pulling back on the reins when she wanted the horse to go forward, resulting in a horse that started backing up whenever there was something he didn't really want to do.

Sitting here reading this, you are probably saying to yourself, "What an idiot, pulling back on the reins when you want to go forward." But you'd be surprised how common that is—how many

Take the Plunge

Horsemanship lesson: You'll learn a safe sequence of steps that will help you introduce your horse to moving water. Then you'll learn how to cross safely.

Why you need it on the trail: As a trail rider, you'll likely encounter a water crossing now and then. Even dry areas can get enough rain to temporarily create water obstacles. You'll show your horsemanship savvy by crossing water safely and purposefully.

I often see riders who think it is fun to jump water or allow their horse to dash to the other side. Jumping water is a great risk, because you can seldom be sure of the footing. It also suggests that your horse is spooked by the water and is moving of his own accord instead of obeying your precise go-forward cues. Plus, it's poor trail etiquette to speed up when the rest of the group is trying to stay at a walk.

I also see riders who allow their horses to paw and play in the water without a correction. This behavior suggests the horses are ready to roll, and I've seen more than one rider unceremoniously dumped in the water this way. While rolling is a bad idea anytime a rider is on board, rolling in moving water puts riders at greater risk for being swept away or ending up in the water under the horse's feet.

What you'll do: Find a riding buddy with a trusty, stream-savvy trail horse who can act as your horse's mentor and stay with you throughout your training session. If you have serious concerns about crossing water with your horse, you may want to have someone pony your horse through the water a few times without you on him.

You'll also need to do some scouting. Find out which water crossings are appropriate for first-time training sessions. As a general guideline, look for a water crossing that's flat and well-traveled by horses or cattle.

If you are riding on private land, you may be able to pick and choose where you'll cross the water and you may be able to find several places to cross repeatedly. On public lands, you may be restricted to designated crossings and you should stay on designated horse trails, to prevent trail erosion. Fortunately, most established crossings are safe and well traveled and your horse will know that other horses have gone there.

The stream shouldn't be too deep or too fast. Look for a water crossing you could walk across yourself without the water reaching above your knees or without a current that would prompt you to lose your balance. Look for clear water that allows you to see the footing on the bottom. Avoid muddy and boggy crossings or ones with too much slick rock or with steep embankments on either side.

Don't use a tie-down or any tack that might prevent your horse from using his head and neck for balance if the water is unexpectedly deep and he needs to swim. Tie-downs or martingales can be lethal if your horse needs to raise his head above water to breathe and he could easily get his legs tangled in straps if he had to swim.

Skills your horse will need: Your horse should be responsive to your cues to move forward, stop, back, and side-to-side. You'll need good steering and speed control at the walk and trot while riding in open spaces. If your horse is familiar with easy trail obstacles (such as crossing poles or logs), you can better trust that he'll go where you ask.

Step 1: Approach With Care

1A

1B

riders pull back on the reins inadvertently when asking the horse to go forward. I see it all the time. Combine the conflicting signal with a horse that doesn't really want to do that anyway, and you end up with a balking, refusing horse. And pulling back on the reins when the horse is backing does not stop him, instead it makes him back faster.

In this case, the rider was very quick to figure out her mistake and, even more impressive, she was able to fix it right away. Problem solved.

Back to water crossings—do you know how to ensure your horse will cooperate every time he's asked to cross a creek or water-filled ditch, or wade into a pond or lake?

This chapter will tell you how.

Water crossings are common on most every trail. But do you and your horse cross without worry or do you ride along the banks, hoping the water will dwindle to a drip?

When you do cross the water, does your horse step forward obediently and quietly, or is he anxious and ready to jump even the smallest puddle? Do you end up pacing back and forth on the bank, poking, prodding, and pleading with your horse to cross?

In this next section, I'll demonstrate the safe and proper way to introduce your horse to a water crossing, then how to cross it slowly and safely. I'll first help you identify the best place to cross. Then I'll show you how to move calmly through the ripples and currents.

Step 1.
Approach With Care

Outfit your horse in his usual riding gear, and ride to your preplanned flat-water crossing. Ask your riding buddy to ride ahead, then follow her to the water's edge (Photo 1A).

2A

2B

When your horse reaches the shoreline, ask him to move forward. Encourage his investigative behavior by reaching your hands forward and applying gentle leg pressure. If he seems curious (as our young horse does in Photo 1B), allow him to sniff and feel the water, then encourage him to move forward and step in. Let him stop with his front feet in the water and allow him to get used to the feel of it before asking him to go all the way in.

As he investigates the water, don't allow your horse to stand and paw at the water—pawing behavior isn't cute and playful, it's a precursor signaling that he's about to lie down to roll. Some horses love to roll in the water.

Let your horse sniff and sip the water if he wants and even play in it with his nose, just be vigilant. If you feel that he's shifting his weight or playing too much, tell him "No!" and pull up on the reins and get him moving.

Also, don't allow your horse to put his head down and rock back on his haunches to jump the creek; jumping water isn't a good trait in a trail horse. If you feel him stretch his neck forward then rock back, sharply correct him with a "whoa" command.

Take all the time you need before you walk your horse into the water. Be patient with him during his investigation as long as he keeps looking at the water and doesn't threaten to turn his nose away or back up.

At this point, you've pointed your horse to the water and expect him to pay attention to the new experience. Insist that his focus stay ahead in the direction you're asking him to go. Don't let him look from right to left because he's looking for a way out of the predicament. His friend and role model should be four to five paces ahead of him, standing in the creek or just on the other side.

It's okay to let your horse stand still, look forward, drink, or sniff, but don't let him turn away or back up. If you do, you'll be training him that water is something to avoid. You'll also be allowing him to choose where he goes, which erodes your control.

Proper Drinking Habits

Chances are, your horse will attempt to drink as you're working on your water-crossing skills. This is the perfect time to instill proper drinking behaviors, as well as water-crossing safety.

Decide what you'd like your horse to do at water crossings when it comes to drinking the water. You might want him to drink at every crossing (left photo) so he'll stay hydrated or to cut down on in-camp watering chores.

Or, you might want your horse to march obediently across the stream without stopping (right photo) to keep the ride moving, drinking only at designated times.

Depending on the type of trail riding you do, you may wish to encourage drinking at every crossing or disallow it. Whatever your idea of perfect water behavior might be, instill it in your horse from the beginning. We prefer to encourage our horses to drink at every crossing, but there are some situations where this may not be a good idea.

Ideally, a young trail horse would be introduced to water in a training environment, with careful attention paid to making it a positive and successful experience. If your horse is not accustomed to going into water, it will pay to plan out his training in as controlled a way as possible. But sometimes we encounter horses who already have a history of problems with water, and either the horse has refused or he has jumped or run across, out of control.

When horses have established bad habits from negative experience, your job will be tougher than what we experienced with this filly, who had no reason to fear water and did not have established bad habits.

If you are dealing with a difficult horse, it may be useful to use an experienced "pony horse" to lead the difficult one into the water. A good pony horse with an experienced rider could even drag an uncooperative horse into the water and go through all the steps outlined above to desensitize a horse to water. But keep in mind, this requires significant skill for both the rider and the pony horse. Sometimes a horse who is really frightened of the water may try to jump on top of the pony horse, and it would be easy for the rider to get knocked off or jerked off the pony horse, if not careful.

If your horse has a history of refusing to cross water or of nervous/fearful behavior, use the techniques outlined in Chapter 11.

Step 2.
Wade and Wait

When your horse seems calm and willing to pay attention to the water's sights and sounds, it's time to move in. Your riding buddy should already be ahead of you and in the stream (Photo 2A). Ask her to stand in the middle of the stream and face upstream with her horse's head in the direction of the water's source so that her horse isn't knocked off balance.

Cue your horse to walk on (Photo 2B). Provide ample rein, and apply gentle, pulsating leg pressure to encourage him to move on.

When you reach the middle of the stream, ask your horse to stop next to his buddy. Relax your body and reins (Photo 2C). Your calm position will show him that the water is a safe and comfortable place to be. You don't want him to learn to rush to the other side.

Hang out for a few minutes until your horse stands quietly. Be patient! This literal "soaking time" will get him used to the sensations of the water and the feel of the bottom and the current.

Even a seasoned trail horse may need to work on this training step. It's important to cross water slowly and precisely so that you can choose the best and least slippery path. And it's important that your horse doesn't rush and plunge across.

Step 3.
Downstream Detour

Now, instead of continuing across the stream to dry land, change direction and ask your horse to calmly walk up and down the waterway along the river bed's length. Spending some time in the water will help him get used to the feel of cold water on his legs and barrel. You'll also reinforce the lesson that you started in Step 2—don't rush.

Step 3: Downstream Detour

He'll learn to step carefully and balance over rocks and uneven terrain that he cannot see.

Spend 5 to 10 minutes walking up and down the stream. Pause every few moments and allow your horse to stand still. Stay in the water until your horse is calm and relaxed. When he seems quiet and confident, it's okay to ride him across and out of the stream at a pace and place you designate.

Make sure the exit from the water is safe and reasonably easy for your inexperienced horse. Steep, slick embankments are scary for a horse and can make him concerned about future water crossings. They also put him at risk for an injury.

Meandering

Question: *My 6-year-old AQHA gelding is very focused in the arena, on or off cattle, keeping his face directed at our target or direction. On the trail, though, he likes to look all around and, if I don't re-direct him, follow his face off toward whatever catches his attention. If I allow that behavior (meandering, I call it), am I creating long-term problems for us? As always, I appreciate your expertise.*

Answer: In defense of your horse, and in the spirit of "you can't have everything," you have to understand that a horse bred to work cattle does not always make the best trail horse. A "cowy" horse's mind is keyed into movement and so he wants to follow it; he notices every little thing and tends to stay on alert. While this works out great in the arena and on cattle, it is not ideal for trail riding. Having said that, being cowy is no excuse for disobedience, and yes, if you allow disobedience it will cause bigger problems for you down the road because it erodes your authority and leadership.

An obedient horse will be focused straight ahead and will go in the direction you ask, at the speed you dictate, without constant direction from you. Many riders micro-manage their horses by constantly steering and correcting speed with the reins, so the horse becomes dependent on that. After you cue a horse to go at a certain speed and in a certain direction, he should continue on that path and at that speed/gait until you ask him to speed up, slow down, turn right, or turn left.

To check how obedient your horse is, find a target and give him a cue to walk or trot straight toward your target, then lay your hand down on his neck with a loose rein, and see if he continues. If he changes speed or direction without a cue from you, it means you have a horse that is either

disobedient or co-dependent on you and you have some work to do. You need to break your habit of micro-managing, give clear directives, then give your horse the responsibility to obey. Correct him with your reins and legs if he makes a mistake; but leave him alone when he is obedient. Use enough pressure in your corrections that he is motivated to behave.

I have written a lot about having nose control on your horse. He should not be looking around while you are riding him, either in the arena or on the trail. Simply correct the nose with the opposite rein—if he looks right, bump the left rein, and vice versa. Do not try to hold the nose in place; just correct it when he is wrong. I use the point of shoulder as a guideline; he can move his nose all he wants as long as it stays between the points of his shoulder; as soon as it crosses the line, he gets a correction. In short order, he will keep his nose pointed in the right direction.

Keep in mind that just because you control the nose, it does not mean you control the rest of the horse. He can easily run through his shoulder and go in the opposite direction that his nose is pointed. The most important thing is to control the horse's shoulder, but if you cannot control the nose, you have little chance of controlling the rest of the body.

How strict I am on the horse's nose and his looking around depends somewhat on the horse, his

level of training, and his willingness to be obedient and subordinate. If I am riding a horse that has proven to be well-behaved, responsive, and obedient, I may let him look around a little, as long as he does not alter the course I have set in either speed or direction. On the other hand, if I have a horse that has proven to be disobedient, spooky, or otherwise fractious, I will have zero tolerance for looking around.

For your cow-bred horse, you will have to factor in his training, temperament, and obedience, and decide how strict you will be. Always correct a horse when he changes course without a cue from you, but with a cowy horse that is bred to be very alert to any movement in his environment, you may have to cut him a little slack as long as he remains obedient.

The most important thing for you is that you have a clear and consistent view of what will be corrected and what is expected of your horse. That's why I use the points of shoulder as a landmark—that way I have clearly defined what I expect and I know exactly when to correct the horse and when not to, so that the horse can clearly understand the rule and that I can give consistent corrections.

For more answers, visit the Training Library: www. juliegoodnight. com/ traininglibrary

Side by Side:
Pony Another Horse Safely Down the Trail

Learn how and why to pony a second horse alongside you while you're on the trail.

Dually and I pony Dodger to demonstrate safe practices.

WHEN MY SON, HUNTER, WAS old enough to ride, I carefully planned his first short trail ride. I had my trusted assistant, Melissa, pony Hunter along, with my horse bringing up the rear so I could keep an eagle eye on him. Ponying is a great way to introduce new horses to the trail—or to keep young or new riders under safe control.

On this day, I admit I learned a lesson about preparing your horse for the trail. While the ponying idea was wonderful, my assistant and I learned an important lesson about tacking up: Only one rider should tack one horse. No tag teaming. On this day, though, my assistant and I both worked in tag-team fashion to saddle Hunter's horse.

Sure enough, whoever was supposed to tighten the girth before we hoisted Hunter up, didn't (we routinely left the cinches loose when we first saddled, and waited until we were ready to mount to tighten them so the horse could be saddled slowly and without too much tension, too fast). With my trusted protégé ponying Hunter on his very nice Welsh-Shetland cross,

I was riding directly behind him on my reliable mare, with the eyes of an eagle on her offspring.

Hunter squealed with delight and chattered and sang the whole way (one of the great joys of life is to watch a young child on his first trail ride, bubbling over with happiness). Approaching our first little hill, I ran my eyes over the pony to check the gear and to my horror, saw there was about two inches of daylight between the cinch and the horse's girth.

Thankfully, Hunter's pony was well trained and had been ponied on the trails many times. He was smooth and steady, and stopped and stood in place as soon as he was asked. We fixed the tack and went on our way with little interruption. If the pony hadn't been used to being handled and hadn't been ponied often, the story may have ended much differently.

Hunter's first trail ride was more than 20 years ago. Since then, I've fine-tuned how to safely pony another horse, and taught it to many of my clients. In this lesson, I'll teach you how.

Simply put, *ponying* means to lead a horse alongside the horse you're riding. It's a technique that's used in all areas of the horse industry from the racetrack, to training barns, to guided trail riding. On the trail, ponying comes in handy when training a new horse, dealing with a pack animal, or leading another rider. As the ponied horse's herd instinct kicks in, he'll likely follow his leader through terrain that might otherwise seem intimidating, such as crossing water. And it's a good way for a young horse to experience potentially spook-inducing, wide-open country without risking a rider's fall.

You might also wish to pony a horse carrying supplies to a campsite, a horse that a child is riding, an injured horse that needs exercise to

Side by Side

Horsemanship lesson: Learn how to safely pony a horse beside you as you ride.

Why you need it on the trail: Ponying a young horse can help expose him to new scenes and experiences before he totes a rider. He'll learn to brave new feats while following a trusted, reliable leader and follow along more willingly than if he were alone. It's also a useful skill in case you need to help a child or injured friend on a long ride. Your horse will also be able to lead a pack animal or an extra horse on pack trips.

What you'll do: You'll learn how to handle the ponied horse's rope, how to cue the ponied horse to move forward, how to teach the ponied horse to stay in position, and how to approach new obstacles while ponying.

What you'll need: If you are going to take a dally on the horn to pony a horse, a saddle with a strong and rigid tree (a flexible tree may apply pressure unevenly across your horse's back if the ponied horse pulls). If you do not plan to dally and will be leading the horse with your right hand, you can ride in a flexible tree. You'll need a bridle for the horse you'll ride; a rope halter and 12-foot lead rope for the horse you'll pony. Wear gloves to protect your hands from rope burns if the ponied horse pulls.

heal, or a horse whose owner has experienced an accident or injury.

In each case, you'll need to know how to pony a horse safely—how to keep you, your horse, and the ponied horse safe. It's a complex task to carefully ride your own horse and guide another horse, all while holding the reins in one hand and a lead rope in the other. Essentially, you are riding two horses—one in each hand, steering your riding horse with your left hand and guiding the other horse with your right hand as he sidles up close, next to your right knee.

But horses don't mind the proximity, because it's natural for them to travel at speed while close to one another and follow the leader (picture a herd of wild mustangs speeding across the plains). Once you know how to handle the ropes, ponying can become a natural, easy way to travel.

Here, I'll teach you how to pony a horse safely while avoiding common pitfalls. You'll learn how to hold a lead rope and reins at the same time, and what to do if the ponied horse moves into an unsafe position. You'll also gain tips to keep the ponied horse moving along at the speed you request.

Before you begin, make sure your *pony horse*—the saddle horse you'll ride—is comfortable with other horses riding nearby. Does he pin his ears or turn away from other horses on group rides? If so, choose another pony horse.

Your pony horse should also be easily controlled with one hand on the reins so you'll have an extra hand to hold onto the ponied horse's lead rope. He should be a safe, reliable mount that doesn't spook.

Your pony horse should also calmly allow ropes to touch his legs and tail, and should drag logs without spooking. These skills will ensure that he won't be bothered by the proximity of another horse and lead rope.

Your ponied horse (the one you'll be leading from horseback) should at least be halter broke and lead well from the ground. To be safe, both horses must have good ground manners and know not to interact with other horses when a human is present.

A rider must be very experienced to pony another horse—it is not a task for just any horse or rider. You'll need to be very balanced at all gaits and very comfortable riding with your left hand. Riding and controlling your horse should be second nature to you because you'll have to focus on controlling the horse you are leading. You'll need to be in pretty good shape physically because you may get jerked around a little. It's very easy when you are ponying another horse to get pulled off balance, have your shoulder jerked back, or have to try to slow down the horse you are leading. If you use a dally on the saddle horn to control the ponied horse, you'll have to be very experienced with ropes, dallies, and how to get out of a tight spot. As I said, this is not for every horse and rider, but ponying is a skill that can come in handy on the trail.

Step 1.
Learn the Ropes

Outfit the horses in the tack listed in the box on page 92. Position the ponied horse on the right side of your pony horse. Move to your pony horse's left side, put the lead rope and reins in your left hand, and mount up. As soon as you're in the saddle and situated, keep the reins in your left hand, but transfer the ponied horse's lead rope to your right hand (Photo 1A).

Note: Always hold the pony horse's rope in a way that you can easily drop it if one horse slips or spooks—never tie or knot the two horses together.

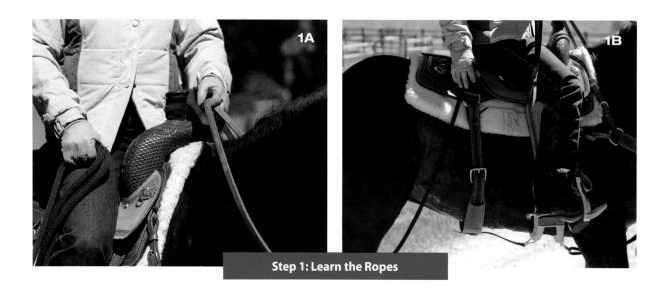

Step 1: Learn the Ropes

Double the lead rope so you can easily lengthen and shorten it. When the lead rope is safely doubled, you'll see a loop in front of your knee as your hand rests on your leg. Never wrap the lead rope around your hand; if the ponied horse pulls or bolts, it could easily pull you off your horse and cause severe injury and or loss of fingers.

Note the doubled rope in my right hand (Photo 1A). The end of the rope nearest to my pinky finger is attached to the horse. The rope extending from my thumb and forefinger is doubled. I'm in position, relaxed, and ready to cue my pony horse by neck reining.

Avoid holding the rope too far behind you (Photo 1B). With this hold and without a doubled rope, too much slack allows your ponied horse to fall far behind your pony horse— precisely in kicking position. The loose rope can also tangle in your pony horse's legs or slip under his tail, potentially causing a wreck.

I will hold this rope and rein position as long as I'm working with a young horse. By holding the rope—instead of fully dallying the rope around the saddle horn—I can cue my ponied

horse to move forward or back. I also ensure that the horses won't be connected if either horse spooks.

When I know my ponied horse is obedient and compliant, I'll often half-loop the lead rope around the saddle horn. This allows me to relax my grip and hold only one piece of the rope. The rope isn't knotted and can quickly be released from the horn. Taking a full dally is highly risky and should only be done by the most accomplished riders on trained pony horses.

Step 2. Go Forward

Ask your pony horse to walk on with your usual rein and leg aids (Photo 2). Include a voice command so that your ponied horse also hears the cue. As your pony horse moves forward, your ponied horse will feel the rope's gentle pull. He should understand these go-forward voice and pressure cues, because he's halter broke.

If your ponied horse doesn't follow along, don't try to pull him forward; you don't have enough strength, and the attempt could wrench your back or pull you off your pony horse.

Instead, stop your pony horse, and take a half-wrap on the saddle horn, holding both ends of the rope in your right hand, down against your leg. Then cue your pony horse forward, and let his body weight pull your ponied horse forward (do this only if you are riding in a rigid-tree saddle). It's pretty easy for the ponied horse to pull against your arm, but he won't pull long against the full weight of the pony horse.

Caveat: To successfully pony a horse, you'll need to have the skill and concentration to deal with two horses at once, such as asking your pony horse to slow down while asking your ponied horse to come forward. Not all riders are ready for this kind of challenge. You might forget to stop your pony horse. Or, you might get pulled off your pony horse by a spooked ponied horse. If you plan to pony a young or unseasoned horse, first practice these initial steps with calm, easygoing horses.

Keep the ponied horse close to your pony horse's hip, with his nose about even with your right knee, so the horses can't step in different directions around a small tree or other obstacle.

Practice walking while maintaining these lead rope and rein holds. First, walk straight ahead, then gradually add turns to the right. Turn only to the right until you're comfortable handling the rope and you can trust your ponied horse to follow. When you turn to the right, you turn toward your ponied horse, enabling the rope to stay in position easily and without causing a pull from the ponied horse.

Turns to the left are tricky if the ponied horse isn't keeping up. Before you turn to the left, make sure your ponied horse is in the correct position; if he falls behind, the lead rope can droop (Photo 1B), touch your pony horse's tail, and even slide up under it, causing your pony horse undue stress and possibly creating a spook.

If the lead rope droops too low or catches on the tail, turn your pony horse back to the right,

Step 2: Go Forward

2

Step 3: Correct Poor Positions

turning the horses nose-to-nose to prevent the rope from wrapping around you; drop the rope at any time, if necessary.

Step 3.
Correct Poor Positions

If your ponied horse falls behind (Photo 1B), simply gather your fingers along the doubled rope to shorten the line, and pull him forward with a bumping action. Your ponied horse should respect this correction, because he knows how to lead from the ground.

Don't allow your ponied horse to move forward so much that he's in front of your knee (Photo 3). You won't have enough leverage to control him, and he can start to lead "the herd" instead of naturally following your pony horse.

If your ponied horse moves too fast and is too forward, pick up your rope-holding hand and jerk it back, pointing your hand in the direction you'd like your ponied horse to be. A quick bump from the rope halter's knot will correct your

ponied horse just as it does during groundwork sessions.

The best pony horses are often good teachers. My pony horse, Dually, knows right where my ponied horse should be. Dually will turn his head and gesture to the ponied horse if he moves up too far.

Step 4.
Move Out

When your ponied horse learns to follow along in formation, moving with your pony horse without needing constant corrections, begin asking both horses for gait changes. Put your horses to work as they transition from walk (Photo 4A) to trot (Photo 4B).

Each time you cue your pony horse, use your verbal cue or a bump of the rope to spur on your ponied horse. Soon, your ponied horse will keep pace, move in step, and easily stay in position.

Ponying another horse is complicated and

requires some getting used to, but it is incredibly helpful, whether you are moving horses to the pasture, leading a pack horse, or training a youngster. If you are totally new to leading another horse while horseback, it's a good

idea to practice first on very broke and well-mannered horses. Start by ponying a new horse in an enclosed area. When you feel like you can control both horses, then it's time to head on down the trail!

Step 4: Move Out

4A

4B

Rope Halter Questions

Question: *My mare is 15 years old and I have NEVER used a rope halter! Do you have a basic "dos and don'ts" for me—things I need to know to help me better understand how it works?*

Answer: There is a lot to know about using rope halters: how they work, how they should fit, and when to use them (and when NOT to use them).

I think of a rope halter as a training aid—it is a way to apply enough pressure on the horse's face to get his attention and/or gain control. It is a far superior tool, in my opinion and experience, than using a stud chain on a horse for control, because you can finesse the pressure with a rope halter. A stud chain will put constant pressure on the horse—you can make the pressure worse but you can never totally release it. With the rope halter, there is only pressure when you manipulate the lead rope, so you have more training ability. But all rope halters are not created equally!

A rope halter can be harsh or mild, depending on the diameter of the rope (thinner is harsher) and the number of knots on the noseband (more knots create more pressure). I prefer to use a thicker diameter stiff rope for my halters and the minimum number of knots to make it a halter. I've yet to meet a horse that wouldn't respond to this amount of pressure, and it is mild enough for everyday use and not just as an aid when you are actively engaged in ground training.

The rope halter should always be adjusted correctly–and make sure you learn how to tie the halter knot right. At the start of every groundwork clinic that I do, I spend a few moments adjusting halters and retying the knots right on the horses in the clinic. A rope halter that hangs too low can

really hurt a horse's nose, and if the noseband were to sag so much that the horse could get a foot in, it could really hurt your horse. Check out this link on my website that explains rope halter fit and how to tie knots correctly. http://juliegoodnight.com/pdf/halterinstructions.pdf

For groundwork, I prefer to use a rope halter (my halters are specially designed for comfort, fit, and effectiveness) and a long training lead, 12 or 15 feet. I do not have metal buckles on my training leads because when I snap the rope, the chin knot will hit the horse in the chin and a metal buckle hitting them can be too much pressure for many horses (they become afraid of the correction and quit thinking). To me, it is critical that the training lead be made of the highest quality marine rope that is soft in your hands and heavy enough to have good feel so that you can make subtle movements with the rope and have an impact on your horse.

As for the DON'TS: never turn a horse loose in a rope halter. For that matter, I wouldn't turn a horse out in any halter but definitely not a rope halter. Generally, they are made of high-tensile rope that will not break; a horse turned loose in a rope halter could catch it on something and get hurt. For the same reason, I would never tie a horse in a trailer in a rope halter. You know he will get off balance at times as you are driving and he'll end up pulling on the halter—I don't want him to have too much pressure on his face just because he got off

balance. Don't use a rope halter that's too snug—there will be constant pressure on his face so you lose the ability to release the pressure. Don't use one that's too big, either; the noseband should not be so large that the horse could get it caught on something.

Tying a horse in a rope halter can be good or it can be a problem if you have a horse that has a pull-back problem. We tie all our yearlings and older horses in rope halters as they are learning to stand tied quietly. They learn not to pull because they'll feel pressure every time they do. But if you have a horse that is a chronic panic puller, the rope halter may make him worse by increasing his panic and fear when he pulls. For more information on this, check out my training library.

An important thing to know before you invest in a rope halter is that all ropes are not created equally and all halters are not tied correctly. With rope products, you get what you pay for. Really high-quality rope that does not stretch, does not break, and works well in your hands is more expensive. You may have already figured this out with cheap lead ropes that break and burn your hands. Also, if not tied correctly, the proportions of the halter can be off so that it never quite fits your horse's face right. As with most equipment that you buy for horses, it is best to stay away from the really cheap stuff.

For more answers, visit the Training Library: www. juliegoodnight. com/ traininglibrary

Epilogue

TRAIL RIDING SEEMS LIKE a casual pursuit, but it still requires good horsemanship skills. As you have seen from the lessons in this book, improving yourself as a rider will not only ease your horse's burden, but it will allow you to have greater control of your horse. Trail riding is all about having fun with your horse in the great outdoors. Being safe and knowing how to do things will help you attain your goals.

Please do your loved ones and me a favor: Wear a helmet when you're working your horse, and especially when you ride out on the trail. Today, helmets are not only safe, but they are comfortable, well fitted, and even stylish, whether out on the trail or in the arena. You wouldn't dream of getting in your car and going somewhere without fastening your seat belt—even though you're not planning to have a wreck today. The same goes for riding your horse, especially out on the trail, where the environment is uncontrolled and the ground is hard. Add to the equation the fact that when you're riding, your head is higher off the ground than in almost any other sport, and you're sitting on an unpredictable,

potentially volatile animal and well, it seems like a no-brainer (pardon the pun).

And remember, whenever you are with horses—just handling them around the barn, loading them in a trailer, or headed out on an extended trail ride—it always pays to keep in mind the worst-case scenario. Try to visualize in advance and predict all the things that can go wrong. In this way, you'll be prepared for any eventuality and both you and your horse will be safer for it. It doesn't take much time to look around and think.

Stay safe, and enjoy the ride. I wish you the best on the trail and everywhere you go!

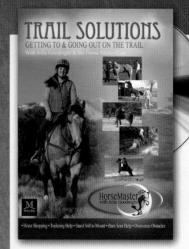

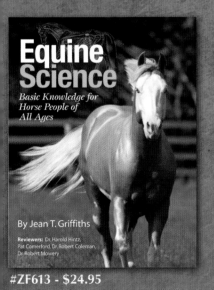
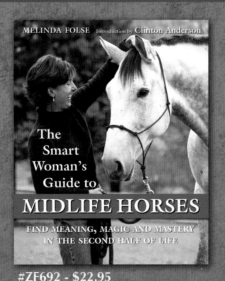